Other Titles in the Smart Pop Series

Taking the Red Pill

Seven Seasons of Buffy

Five Seasons of Angel

What Would Sipowicz Do?

Stepping through the Stargate

The Anthology at the End of the Universe

Finding Serenity

The War of the Worlds

Alias Assumed

Navigating the Golden Compass

Farscape Forever!

Flirting with Pride and Prejudice

Revisiting Narnia

Totally Charmed

King Kong Is Back!

Mapping the World of Harry Potter

The Psychology of The Simpsons

The Unauthorized X-Men

The Man from Krypton

Welcome to Wisteria Lane

The Battle for Azeroth

Star Wars on Trial

Boarding the Enterprise

Getting Lost

www.smartpopbooks.com

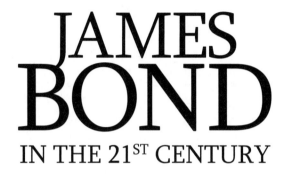

JAMES BOND

IN THE 21ST CENTURY

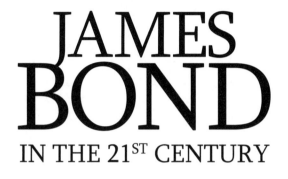

JAMES BOND
IN THE 21ST CENTURY

JAMES BOND

IN THE 21ST CENTURY

WHY WE STILL NEED
007

EDITED BY
Glenn Yeffeth
WITH **Leah Wilson**

BENBELLA BOOKS, INC.
Dallas, Texas

BenBella Books, Inc.
6440 N. Central Expressway, Suite 617
Dallas, TX 75206
www.benbellabooks.com
Send feedback to feedback@benbellabooks.com

Printed in the United States of America
10 9 8 7 6 5 4 3 2 1

Library of Congress Cataloging-in-Publication Data

James Bond in the 21st century : why we still need 007 / edited by Glenn Yeffeth, with Leah Wilson.
    p. cm.
    ISBN 1-933771-02-X
    1. James Bond films--History and criticism. 2. Bond, James (Fictitious character) I. Yeffeth, Glenn, 1961–
II. Wilson, Leah.

PN1995.9.J3J36 2006
791.43'75—dc22

                                                                                        2006015748

Proofreading by Stacia Seaman and Zachary Settle
Cover design by Todd Michael Bushman
Text design and composition by John Reinhardt Book Design
Printed by Victor Graphics, Inc.

Distributed by Independent Publishers Group
To order call (800) 888-4741
www.ipgbook.com

For media inquiries and special sales contact Yara Abuata at yara@benbellabooks.com

Contents

How to Make James Bond Your Bitch

INTERLUDE: Dress Like Bond

James Bond in the 21st Century

THE REAL
JAMES BOND

Can the Cinematic Bond Ever Be the Literary Bond?

JAMES BOND IS NOT a nice guy. He's often irritable and broods a great deal about his life and profession. Bond drinks too much, smokes too much, gambles too much, and treats women cold-heartedly and ruthlessly. He keeps to himself most of the time but overly indulges in the sensory pleasures that food, drink, tobacco, and sex give him because he knows that on any given day he may no longer be alive. Bond is good looking, but in a cold, cruel way, and he has a scar down his right cheek. He has no taste in art, music, theater, or film. Other than newspapers, whatever he reads is usually for his work—manuals on self-defense and the like—although he's been known to pick up an old Eric Ambler thriller for plane trips. He's painfully set in his ways, looks at the world with cynicism, has relatively no sense of humor, and can claim very few friends.

Not the image of James Bond you usually imagine? Unless you've read the original Ian Fleming novels then that's most likely the case, for this is a fairly accurate description of the character as depicted in the books.

It's no wonder that Ian Fleming found it very difficult for his literary creation to make the transition from the page to the silver screen. For nearly ten years, the author was concerned that James Bond might not become a film commodity at all.

3

The Long Road to the Big Film Deal

Ever since the first novel, *Casino Royale*, was published in the United Kingdom in 1953 (and in the United States in 1954), Fleming always envisioned a movie version of 007. Despite early sales of film rights and nibbles from Hollywood throughout the rest of that decade, however, the big movie deal eluded the author.

The first important early sale went to CBS television in 1954, shortly after the publication of the novel in America. The rights were sold to make a one-hour adaptation for the network's *Climax!*, a dramatic series of mystery and suspense adaptations taped live in the studio. Broadcast in October of that year, *Casino Royale* starred Barry Nelson as American "Jimmy" Bond, Peter Lorre as the villain Le Chiffre, and Linda Christian as the first Bond girl, Vesper Lynd. Needless to say, Nelson's television character had little to do with Fleming's literary creation other than he liked martinis and was an excellent card sharp. The teleplay, however, faithfully followed the novel's plot, albeit toned down for American audiences and the network censors.

Producer Gregory Ratoff bought the feature motion picture rights to *Casino Royale* in 1955 but did nothing with the property, sitting on it until his death in 1960. Ratoff's widow promptly sold the rights to Hollywood agent-turned-producer Charles K. Feldman, who also left the property undeveloped until late in the '60s, after the "official" film series produced by EON Productions had been underway for five years and was a runaway success. *Casino Royale* finally made it to the screen in 1967, but very little about it had much to do with Ian Fleming's original creation. Feldman, capitalizing on his 1965 "mod comedy" hit *What's New, Pussycat?* and fearing that he couldn't compete with the EON series, decided to make *Casino Royale* as a spoof of Bond and spy movies in general. The likes of Peter Sellers, David Niven, Woody Allen, Orson Welles, Ursula Andress, and Joanna Pettet starred in the picture, which critics and fans found to be a complete mess. It was neither funny nor coherent. It did, however, sport a lively and popular score by Burt Bacharach. But a Bond movie it wasn't.

A little later in 1955, Fleming sold the film rights to his third Bond novel, *Moonraker*, to the Rank Organization. Once again, the film company did nothing with the property, and Fleming eventually bought the rights back in 1959. The author was learning that the motion picture business was not an easy nut to crack.

Fleming toyed with other film possibilities during the '50s. During the summer of 1956 he was approached by NBC to develop a television series provisionally called *Commander Jamaica*. It was to be an adventure program filmed in the Caribbean, the author's stomping grounds and often a location for Bond stories, except that the main character was to be named James Gunn. Fleming wrote a treatment for the pilot but the project fell apart by the end of the year. Instead, Fleming used the basic plot of the treatment for his next 007 novel, *Dr. No*.

In early 1958 Fleming was approached once again by an American television network, this time CBS, to write thirty-two episodes for a James Bond television series. The author accepted the offer and worked on the first few outlines until this venture also fell by the wayside. Once again, Fleming retained some of the plot outlines and developed them into Bond short stories that were published in the 1960 anthology *For Your Eyes Only*.

Fleming's desire to bring James Bond to the screen was nearly squashed altogether when he entered into a partnership that would have disastrous results. The author's lifelong (and wealthy) friend Ivar Bryce had become a film producer. Bryce had formed Xanadu Productions with a young filmmaker named Kevin McClory. McClory was interested in making the first James Bond motion picture, but he was adamant that the film be based on an original screenplay and not one of Fleming's existing books. Thus, in the spring of 1959, Fleming, McClory, Bryce, and their friend Ernest Cuneo brainstormed about a possible plot in which two nuclear bombs are stolen by a criminal organization and used to collect ransom from the superpowers. Cuneo wrote a short outline which became the basis for *James Bond of the Secret Service*, the first original screenplay featuring 007. Fleming tried his hand at writing the first script and its subsequent revision but quickly realized that film writing was not his forte. McClory brought in a professional screenwriter, Jack Whittingham, to rewrite and polish the script. The project underwent a title change to *Longitude 78 West*, until Fleming made an executive decision and re-named it *Thunderball*. The story is notable for introducing the villainous organization SPECTRE and its leader, Ernst Stavro Blofeld.

Unfortunately, McClory's independent film produced by Bryce, *The Boy and the Bridge*, wasn't faring well. Fleming and Bryce apparently lost faith in the filmmaker. As McClory's efforts to interest a major studio in the project dragged into 1960, Fleming simply lost interest. Feeling that the movie project had died like all the others, he went on to write his next 007 novel and naïvely—and recklessly—incorporated the *Thunderball* plot. When the novel was published in 1961, Kevin McClory sued for plagiarism. In the 1963 court settlement, McClory gained ownership of the *Thunderball* film rights.

By that time, of course, the official series by EON Productions was in full swing. In late 1960, Canadian producer Harry Saltzman became interested in the Bond novels and in 1961 bought an option for all the existing titles (which excluded *Casino Royale*, since it had already been sold). Unbeknownst to him, London-based American producer Albert R. "Cubby" Broccoli also had become keen on producing a series of films based of Fleming's books but was stonewalled when he discovered that Saltzman had the option. The two men decided to join forces and produce the films together. They formed DANJAQ S.A., the holding company that governed the team's production company, EON. At first the producers picked *Thunderball* to be the first film but had to abandon the idea when the novel came under litigation. *Dr. No* became its replacement.

From Page to Screen—Changes and Innovations

While the search for an actor to play James Bond went forward, veteran Hollywood screenwriter Richard Maibaum adapted the novel to the screen (with the help of Johanna Harwood and Berkley Mather). From the onset, the producers felt that more humor needed to be injected into the stories. Broccoli and Saltzman wisely perceived that Fleming's brooding and cold misanthrope wouldn't play well to theater audiences of the early '60s. Hence, the cinematic Bond became a more sophisticated man-of-the-world with considerable knowledge in a variety of subjects. He also became a witty deliverer of sardonic quips as he dispatched adversaries and bedded voluptuous girlfriends. The decision was also made, especially beginning with the second film, *From Russia with Love*, to incorporate high-tech gadgetry into the series. The '60s was a decade in which electronics advancement skyrocketed, so it was only natural that an international secret agent should come equipped with all manner of outrageous—but possible—accoutrement. Fleming had experimented a little with spy hardware in the books, but not as extensively as the films eventually did. A trick attaché case is one thing; a hovercraft gondola in Venice is something else altogether.

The actor cast in the coveted role was Sean Connery, a relatively unknown Scot who had starred in a few forgettable pictures in the late '50s and very early '60s. What impressed the producers about him was his "animal magnetism." In truth, Connery was dissimilar to Fleming's literary character in many ways. Fleming's Bond was more of an upper-crust Etonian type (although Bond never finished his schooling at Eton), whereas Connery was decidedly Scot working class. Fleming had grave reservations. His idea of Bond was that of a young David Niven.

6

Enter Terence Young, the director of *Dr. No.* Young, a very sophisticated and adventurous man himself, took Connery under his wing and proceeded to educate the actor in the ways of being dapper, witty, and, above all, cool. Young escorted Connery around London, introducing him to the high life, the gambling parlors, the fancy restaurants, and the women. By the time shooting for *Dr. No* began in January 1962, Connery was ready. And Fleming was surprised and pleased to see what the filmmakers had done with his character. He was so impressed by Connery's portrayal that he indicated in subsequent novels that Bond was "half-Scottish," something to which he had never before alluded.

The first two Bond films, *Dr. No* (1962) and *From Russia with Love* (1963), were the only two that Ian Fleming saw. It was fortunate for him that these two pictures were more or less faithful in concept and storyline to his original novels. Sean Connery was not exactly the James Bond of the books, but he was nevertheless handsome, charismatic, and exciting. Much of the success of the early films can be attributed to Connery's instant star power, although it would be negligent not to mention that the pictures exhibited a wholly original *style* created by director Young, writer Maibaum, and editor Peter Hunt. Throw in the spectacular science fiction sets by production designer Ken Adam and the signature theme music composed by Monty Norman (and subsequent scores by John Barry) and the Bond films immediately became something very new in the action thriller genre. But when asked by reporters what he had thought of *Dr. No* after its premiere in London, Fleming implied that while it was a very good picture, anyone who had read the book would likely be disappointed.

Film historians might argue that it was the third Bond film, *Goldfinger*, released in 1964 shortly after Fleming's death, that became the blueprint for the continuing EON series. A new director, Guy Hamilton, injected even more humor into the proceedings. In *Goldfinger*, the tone slyly poked fun at itself, as if the filmmakers were winking at the audience. For example, Bond's first appearance involved emerging from water with a fake duck atop his scuba headpiece. When 007 pushed that red button ("Whatever you do, don't touch it!" warned Q) and the Aston-Martin's ejector seat sent the Korean guard flying, the audience couldn't help but scream with laughter. "This is all for fun, folks, so enjoy the ride," the filmmakers seemed to be saying. And it worked. *Goldfinger* was the first Bond film that *really* brought in the gold, so to speak. This was the picture that made James Bond and Sean Connery household names around the world. Suddenly, pop culture went secret agent–crazy. Bond imitations popped up everywhere—on television, in the cinemas, in comics, in books, and even in commercials. The mid-'60s displayed an onslaught of spy entertainment, from *The Man from U.N.C.L.E.*, *I Spy*, *Secret Agent*, and *Get Smart* on television, to the Matt Helm and Derek Flint pictures in theaters. But it was James Bond who led the pack.

The End of the Classic Period

Aficionados agree that the Bond films of the '60s represented the "Classic" period of 007 onscreen. Even though Sean Connery announced his retirement from the role of 007 after the blockbusters *Thunderball* (1965) and *You Only Live Twice* (1967), there was to be one more entry in the series that fell within this Classic period.

In 1968 the producers held yet another talent search to re-cast the now world-renowned secret agent and came up with Australian George Lazenby, an unknown male model who had never acted before. He certainly looked the part and probably could have grown into the role if given the chance. It didn't hurt that Peter Hunt, the new director, wanted to film *On Her Majesty's Secret Service* as faithfully to Fleming's novel as he could, including the downbeat ending in which Bond's new wife is murdered within an hour of the wedding. The film, released in 1969, was not a success. Lazenby, who had more or less done a Sean Connery imitation, was let go, Hunt was dismissed, and Broccoli and Saltzman did everything they could to woo Connery back to the role one more time for 1971's *Diamonds Are Forever*. What is interesting to note is that today the hardcore James Bond fans regard *On Her Majesty's Secret Service* to be one of the best films in the series, if not *the* best. Lazenby's performance has been reevaluated, the picture itself is deemed the most accurate representation of a Fleming novel onscreen, and it is now considered one of the great, classic Bond films.

A New Decade and a New Type of Bond Film

Guy Hamilton returned to helm Connery's one-time return for *Diamonds Are Forever*, and this time the director imbued the film with more humor than ever before, sometimes dipping into slapstick. After the financial failure of *On Her Majesty's Secret Service,* the producers must have dictated that the new Bond film be more of an "entertaining romp" than a serious spy picture. Audiences apparently loved the result, for *Diamonds Are Forever* brought the grosses back on track. And Connery said goodbye once more.

English actor Roger Moore took over the role and slipped into this new style of Bond picture with ease. The movies themselves veered directly into what could be called "action comedies" rather than "action thrillers." Everything was played for laughs, even the eye-popping stunts and set pieces. Fleming's Bond character virtually disappeared, replaced by a pinball bouncing between the various action sequences that attempted to form some semblance of a plot. Roger Moore held court in this position for a total of seven movies over thirteen years. While he may have been suitable to play Bond by appearance and background alone, Roger Moore turned the character into a rather smarmy, eyebrow-raising international playboy who never seemed to get hurt.

Perhaps the filmmakers felt that Bond had already become a parody of himself by this time. Did audiences fail to take James Bond seriously anymore? Were laughs, big stunts, huge set pieces, and gadgets the only bankable elements of a 007 film in the '70s? Whatever the answers to these questions might be, there is no argument to the fact that Roger Moore's Bond films made even more money than those of the '60s.

One interesting development occurred in 1983—during the Roger Moore era—and it involved none other than Sean Connery and the filmmaker who had originally collaborated with Ian Fleming on the *Thunderball* screenplay from the late '50s. After legally winning the film rights to the property in 1963, Kevin McClory made a deal with EON producers Broccoli and Saltzman to co-produce *Thunderball* as the fourth EON James Bond film (McClory received full producer credit). McClory retained the remake rights and he attempted to exercise them a few times during the '70s but EON's powerful lawyers threw obstacles in his way until 1982, when McClory joined forces with independent producer Jack Schwartzman. Together, they managed to convince a studio to remake *Thunderball*. Entitled *Never Say Never Again*, the picture was released as a rival film, by a rival production company, to compete with EON's then current picture, *Octopussy*. McClory and Schwartzman even had an ace up their sleeve—Connery—who agreed to play Bond again in the renegade movie. And while *Never Say Never Again* may have been a more faithful representation of the "early" Bond films and even Fleming's *Thunderball* novel, it lacked the glitz, glamour, and important trademark elements of the EON series such as the opening "gunbarrel" logo and familiar Bond theme music. Reception was mixed.

New Attempts to Re-Imagine Fleming's Bond

Albert R. Broccoli was, by the mid-'80s, producing the series alone with the help of his stepson, Michael G. Wilson, and it was felt that a change in tone was needed. After Roger Moore had aged out of the role, an attempt was made to bring Bond back down to earth and make some serious spy adventures once again. Timothy Dalton, a noted Welsh actor with impressive stage and screen credits, was cast as 007 for *The Living Daylights*, released in 1987. Dalton reportedly read all of Fleming's books to prepare for the role and insisted on playing the character as faithfully as possible. As a result, the Bond of *Daylights* and its follow-up, *Licence to Kill* (1989), was not what audiences were accustomed to seeing. Dalton purposefully played Bond as a ruthless and serious man with very little of the wit displayed by Connery, Lazenby, or Moore. While the films were moderately successful, audiences sent a clear message to the filmmakers that these were not the kind of Bond movies they wanted to see, even though the purist fans embraced them wholeheartedly.

By the mid-'90s, EON Productions was forced to re-invent James Bond once again. Dalton was out and Pierce Brosnan was in. The first Irish Bond, Brosnan seemed to be the perfect choice. He was already popular as a result of his television stint in *Remington Steele*, had charisma, and was popular with the ladies. But there was a different problem besides casting—EON Productions had run out of Ian Fleming stories to adapt (*The Living Daylights* was the last Fleming title to be filmed). In actuality, the last Fleming *story* that was recognizable on the screen was *On Her Majesty's Secret Service*. The filmmakers tended to use the titles, character names, and sometimes the locations from Fleming's books—but very little of the original plots—in the pictures of the '70s and '80s.

With Michael G. Wilson and Cubby Broccoli's daughter Barbara acting as the co-producers of the series, EON began rolling out James Bond merchandise. Competition with major Hollywood action blockbusters pushed the filmmakers into making the Bond films bigger, louder, and more explosive, not to mention loaded with product placements. Thus, the four films made with Pierce Brosnan between 1995 and 2002 suffer from overkill. With the emphasis on action and special effects, the storytelling often became too complicated and curiously lacking in suspense—quite a departure from the Classic period films of the '60s. The audiences still came in droves, though—apparently the eye candy was enough to sustain James Bond as a commodity into the twenty-first century.

James Bond Comes Full Circle

At the time of this writing, EON Productions has made yet another change. A new actor, Daniel Craig, was cast as 007 in 2005 in preparation for the next film to be released in 2006—and ironically, the title is *Casino Royale* (the rights to which EON ultimately secured). After fifty-three years, Ian Fleming's first James Bond novel is finally making it to the screen in a serious format—as promised by the filmmakers, anyway—so *perhaps* audiences will see the author's original conception onscreen. The filmmakers undoubtedly have the opportunity to deliver it, but will they truly go for a serious and faithful adaptation? The Bond fan purists will assuredly welcome the picture, but will the general public accept it?

The problem is that "James Bond" has become so many different things to audiences around the world. There are those who believe Bond is the tough, sardonic, and sexy Sean Connery. Slightly younger people prefer the coolly sophisticated and humorous Roger Moore. Still others prefer the action man who successfully incorporated a little of every Bond actor that preceded him—Pierce Brosnan. And yet, the *true* Bond aficionados— the readers of Ian Fleming's original books—see Bond as the cold, brooding spy Fleming created, a completely different entity than what has been portrayed at the cinema.

Perhaps it's too late for filmmakers to ever "win" when it comes to 007. The character certainly comes with a lot of gadgets, loves, and scars…but he also comes with a tremendous amount of baggage.

Between 1996 and 2002, **RAYMOND BENSON** was commissioned by the James Bond literary copyright holders to take over writing the 007 novels. In total he penned and published worldwide six original 007 novels (including *Zero Minus Ten* and *The Man with the Red Tattoo*), three film novelizations, and three short stories. His classic encyclopedic work on the 007 phenomenon, *The James Bond Bedside Companion*, was first published in 1984 and was nominated for an Edgar Allan Poe Award by Mystery Writers of America for Best Biographical/Critical Work. Raymond has also written non-Bond novels: *Face Blind* (2003) and *Evil Hours* (2004). Using the pseudonym "David Michaels," Raymond is also the author of the bestselling books *Tom Clancy's Splinter Cell* (2004) and its sequel *Tom Clancy's Splinter Cell—Operation Barracuda* (2005), both *New York Times* bestsellers. Raymond's most recent original suspense novel is *Sweetie's Diamonds*, published in 2006. www.raymondbenson.com

JOHN COX

The Sexual Subtext of 007
Or, Why We (Really) Like These Movies

GOOD FILMS HAVE SUBTEXT. What do I mean by subtext? On the surface *Raiders of the Lost Ark* is a movie about an archeologist seeking to find the biblical Ark of the Covenant before the Nazis do. That's its text. But is that really what *Raiders of the Lost Ark* is *about*? Is this basic "plot" enough to tap into the worldwide public consciousness and produce a phenomenon? No way. What makes *Raiders* resonate, the reason we find ourselves saying, "That was a really good movie," is that we are having an unconscious reaction to the film's subtext. *Raiders of the Lost Ark* is really about an atheist's search for God. Now, you're not necessarily supposed to know this is what the film is about, but you are supposed to feel it. It's one of the ways movies manipulate you emotionally. And despite what some people will argue, good filmmakers use subtext the way they use lighting. It's all very specific and intentional but designed to be invisible.

As a rule, subtext is communicated with metaphors. To continue with the *Raiders* example: In the beginning, when confronted with any mention of spirituality, Indy flatly says he doesn't believe in "all that hocus-pocus" and even calls the lightning coming from the Ark "the power of God *or something*" [emphasis mine]. The screenwriters communicate Indy's disbelief (or at least skepticism) without ever using the word *atheist*. But the

Ark can prove the existence of God; therefore, metaphorically, the Ark is God. By the end of the film, Indy commits the ultimate act of faith by closing his eyes when the Ark is opened. "Don't look at it!" he screams to Marion. Indy demonstrates that he does not seek proof. He *believes*, and, thus, God spares his life.

Now, if *Raiders of the Lost Ark* were just about the search for an archeological relic, the ending would be a letdown. After all, Indy loses the Ark. But that's not the feeling we have at the end of *Raiders*, because the real story has been resolved. Indy has found his faith, and spiritual unity with his long-lost love, Marion.

Such is the subtextual journey of Dr. Jones. What about Mr. Bond? Is subtext at work in the 007 films, or are these just "spy" films devoid of deeper meaning? The fact that these movies are so ritualized and continue to be compelling decades later tells us they are not simple spy movies. There's more going on . . . much more.

So let's examine what I see as deep subtext in three classic James Bond films: *You Only Live Twice, From Russia with Love,* and the prototypical Bond film, *Goldfinger.* Warning: What follows may forever change the way you look at these three films. Like Indy, you don't have to believe in all this "hocus-pocus" for it to be real. I'm going to open the Ark, and it's up to you whether you close your eyes or have a look inside.

You Only Live Twice: James Bond Goes to Hell

You Only Live Twice is a perfect title for this fifth James Bond adventure. After the megapic *Thunderball*, where else could Bond go but to the afterworld? Yes, beneath its surface text, *You Only Live Twice* is a movie about James Bond's death and journey through purgatory. Never has a world seemed so out of Bond's control; yet never has Bond seemed so utterly resigned to his fate. "I just might retire to here," he tells Tiger. If you think I'm reading too much into *You Only Live Twice*, you only have to be reminded that the author of the screenplay is Roald Dahl, who wrote such psychedelic hero's journeys as *Charlie & the Chocolate Factory* and *James & the Giant Peach.*

You Only Live Twice starts in very familiar territory with 007 in bed with a beautiful woman. The end of most Bond movies is the beginning of this one. Except his companion is Asian, a fact unusual enough for Bond to comment on it: "Why do Chinese girls taste different from all other girls?" His instincts that there may be something "off-taste" about his latest conquest prove correct when she turns out to be his very own Angel of Death.

14

Gunmen sweep into the room, and Bond is killed before our eyes. "At least he died on the job," says the police officer on the scene. We then drift into the title sequence. But are we seeing puffy clouds and harps? No. We're in a world of volcanoes, fire, and lava. James Bond is on his way to Hell.

The movie then opens with Commander Bond's burial at sea. The movie, as a metaphor, begins here as 007's corpse is retrieved by two divers (flying angels) who bring it not back to the surface but aboard a submarine (the first of many phallic symbols in this film). "Permission to come aboard?" asks Bond.

After a briefing—where, notably, M and the rest of the SIS staff are dressed in white uniforms while Bond is in black—007 is ejected from the sub's torpedo tube. (007 as sperm? Sure, why not?) Bond then surfaces into a world that's entirely unfamiliar to him, a world in which he is constantly trapped and fooled, usually by women. In this strange upside-down world, Bond is called "Zero Zero" instead of 007, and even his martini order is mysteriously reversed, "stirred, not shaken." Oddly enough, Bond confirms the mix as "perfect." Bond admits to Tiger Tanaka that he's never been to Japan, which is odd for a man as worldly as James Bond— and didn't he mention an affair with "Ann in Tokyo" in *From Russia with Love*? Also revealing is the fact that *You Only Live Twice* is the only single location Bond film. There's no globetrotting here. James Bond is stuck.

Things get even more surreal when Bond must "become Japanese." Bond is operated on in a womblike room, married, and given a home in a pearl diving village where, strangely enough, he seems perfectly content. He's moved another ring closer to his final resting place. But a violent reminder of his own death (again in a bed) snaps Bond out of his passivity, and it's off to the volcanic lair of the villain. Here, for reasons not fully explained, Bond thinks the answer to the crisis at hand is to go into outer space. A natural instinct to ascend into the heavens, perhaps? But just as Bond is about to finally leave his purgatory, the master of the volcano recognizes him and shouts, "Stop that astronaut!"

It's appropriate that Ernst Stravo Blofeld is seen for the first time in *You Only Live Twice*. Up to this point in the series, Blofeld has been only an unseen, omniscient presence, ordering other men to commit his evil deeds while stroking a cat (cats are traditionally the guardians of the underworld). The clearest metaphor of the film is that Blofeld is the Devil. After all, who else would live in a volcano? When facing Blofeld, Bond pretty much verbalizes the subtext of the film. "Yes, this is my second life," he says.

Of course, it all ends in a fiery explosion caused not by Bond but by Blofeld—and Bond finds himself back where he was at the end of *Thunder-*

ball: in a raft with a bikini-clad woman. Back to the familiar world of 007. Back to the surface. Resurrection.

From Russia with Love: Sex and the Secret Agent

Is *From Russia with Love* a great spy film? Yes, but there is more—much more. Like the original novel, *From Russia with Love* is really a catalog of "secret" sexual fetishes thinly veiled by the world of the '60s Secret Agent.

Think about it. *From Russia with Love* depicts sadism (making two fish fight to the death); oil massage (Grant on SPECTRE Island); S&M (Klebb's handy riding crop and brass knuckles); pimp prostitution (Bond and Tatiana are both, essentially, employed to have sex); erotomania (Tatiana falls in love with a photo of Bond "like young girls fall in love with movie stars"); lesbianism (Tatiana's "interview" with Klebb); polygamy (Kerim's multiple children suggest multiple wives); exotic dancing (in this case, belly dancing); erotic wrestling (the Gypsy catfight—more on this later); ménage a trois (Bond is delivered both gypsy girls to his tent); bondage (the dead Prussian in the back of the Renault is very well tied); oral sex (Tatiana's mouth is just the "right size" for Bond); voyeurism (the men watch Bond and Tatiana as they secretly film them, among *many* other examples); public exhibitionism (Tatiana wants to wear her nightgown "in Piccadilly"); sadomasochistic homosexuality (the Grant-Bond confrontation); and yes, even foot worship (how else can you account for the appeal of that spike-tipped shoe or Grant's insistence that Bond "Crawl over here and kiss my foot!"). Much of this comes from the novel, and it's no secret that Fleming enjoyed a taste of the whip from time to time.

The gypsy girl fight is *From Russia with Love*'s most infamous scene of pure sadism. Never has a Bond movie felt so much like a snuff film. Where most movies poke fun at "catfights," this film puts it on a level of a gladiatorial match. They don't say the girls are fighting to death, but they don't say they aren't! In fact, the fight between the two women "in love with the same man" is so savage (or so arousing?) that Bond asks for it to be stopped. Strange that the only way we're "saved" from this scene is by an explosion of good old-fashioned gunplay. Stranger yet is the relief we feel at the arrival of this "safe" movie violence. How sexually charged is this scene? When *From Russia with Love* aired on ABC throughout the '70s and '80s, the entire gypsy camp sequence was cut from the film. I doubt this was because of the belly dancer.

Related to the gypsy fight in its depiction of sexual violence uncommon in a Bond film is Bond hitting Tatiana in real anger aboard the Orient

16

Express. It's interesting to note that Bond is posing as her husband at the time. Her crime? She lied to him. Dark.

But the confrontation with Red Grant is the ultimate ordeal for James Bond in this sexually lethal world. Of all sexual terrors, being on the end of a homosexual rape certainly ranks high. The lead-up to the fight is highly charged with innuendoes. Grant has clearly been aroused by the footage of Bond and Tatiana's lovemaking. A line that exists in the continuity script but is missing from existing prints has Grant saying, "What a performance!" Grant makes Bond get on his knees (waist level) and tells him it'll be "painful and slow." Let's not forget that this whole confrontation is taking place in a train compartment (read *bunk*, read *bed*). And what's the first thing that goes when they start their "struggle"? The light. There's an orgasmic quality to Grant's silent death, but maybe I should stop here before I lose the family audience—which, by the way, is what the movie does as well. In the book, the Grant-Bond fight is the climax of the story and rightfully so. But the filmmakers felt compelled to give us a helicopter and boat chase, which dilute the sexual subtext of the film. But maybe that's the intent. After all, sometimes a boat chase is just a boat chase.

Goldfinger: James Bond and the Oedipus Complex

When you get right down to it, James Bond films are modern representations of what Freud called the Oedipal stage of development—namely, the unconscious anxiety male adolescents deal with when challenging their all-powerful fathers in a struggle to find their own way in the world and, most importantly, emerge with their own women, their reward for completing the Oedipal "mission." That's why the best Bond villains must be older than Bond, and why Bond films first appeal to boys at around age fourteen.

It's in adolescence that we play out our own inner Oedipal/separation dramas, and Bond films help us deal with the exotic "outside" world. As with fairy tales, we repeat the basic story over and over without variation and until we "grow out of" them. That's why some older Bond fans feel the Bond films "stopped working" after some particular point/film in their past. It's not that the films stopped working (that's obvious from all the new fans), it's that older viewers are no longer able to connect emotionally with the films on this most powerful subtextual level. So which film best displays this Oedipal subtext in its most archetypal form? That's simple. It's the film that's frequently held up as the archetype of all Bond films—*Goldfinger*.

Incredibly, *Goldfinger* starts off with Bond admitting to cabaret dancer Bonita, "I have a slight inferiority complex." Sure, he's making a quip, but it's a strange quip for James Bond to make. By having Bond say this, the filmmakers establish the very existence of psychological "complexes" in the world of James Bond. Furthermore, at its root, an "inferiority complex" is an Oedipal complex. So you have to ask, "To whom does Bond feel inferior?" You only need to look at the title of the film to find the answer.

Auric Goldfinger is clearly a father figure and Bond clearly a "son" in this film. Just compare their cars. Both cars are British but clearly of a different era. Goldfinger drives a chauffeur-driven Rolls Royce, old-world power derived from wealth. Bond drives a brand-new Aston Martin DB5, a symbol of "youthful" sexual power. In fact, Bond's car is more than sexual; it's turned into an object of fetish via amazing gadgets. The only extra on Goldfinger's Rolls is Oddjob, and yes, Oddjob is the physical representative of Goldfinger's sexual power. But more on this later.

The core of the Oedipal drama is the hero's/son's relationship to women and the danger/anxiety he faces when stepping into this most sacred realm of Daddy's sexual power—going after his "gold," so to speak. *Goldfinger* goes out of its way to play every beat of this subtextual theme. In fact, the inciting incident of *Goldfinger* is not a massive crime or a compelling mystery, but the massive Oedipal mistake Bond makes in sleeping with Goldfinger's woman (metaphorical Mommy). The love scene in Bond's hotel suite seems more domesticated than normal. He's trying on the role of husband, i.e., "Father." I mean, have we even seen Bond in a kitchen before? And Bond's Beatle remark ("That's like listening to the Beatles without earmuffs") seems out of character. Complaining about rock-and-roll music is something an old man does, not a young, modern man like James Bond. This is also the last thing Bond says before he's knocked unconscious by a mysterious hand (the phantom hand of Daddy Wrath?).

When Bond awakes, he is presented with the most famous image in all Bond history: Jill has been killed. More than killed, she has been reclaimed, smothered by Goldfinger's power (his gold), and turned into his eternal object. Goldfinger is sending a powerful message to Bond here: *Dead or alive, this woman is mine.* Bond is truly shaken by this, and for the rest of film, he will tread very lightly around women.

Almost secondary to Bond's psychodrama is the plot (text) of *Goldfinger*. "This isn't a personal vendetta, 007," warns M. But, of course, it is, because Bond's official mission is perfectly in line with his Oedipal mission. Find out where Daddy gets his power—his gold. Gold/money clearly symbolizes adult power in this film, a power that Bond *doesn't* have. "You'll draw it from Q Branch in the morning," scolds M when Bond reaches for the bar of Nazi gold at the Bank of England (yet another symbol of old-world power). Moneypenny even reminds us that wedding rings are made of gold. She does this, by the way, as she deftly tosses Bond's hat onto the hat rack—a demonstration of power usually reserved for Bond. Powerful, in-control women abound in *Goldfinger*; it's one of the reasons the film feels so contemporary.

One thing that has always amazed me about the Bond-Goldfinger relationship is that they fully know what each is trying to do to the other, yet they engage in a sort of bizarre civil dance. It's not unlike a rebellious teen who sits at his father's dinner table, secretly wishing to stab him with a steak knife, and the father who accepts his son's murderous intent because he knows the son is not yet "man enough" to take him. Therefore, Father and Son do "battle" via sports. In *Goldfinger* they play golf. And what's the prize? Gold (and all it represents). But we know the gold bar is not Bond's to gamble with. It's a dangerous bluff on Bond's part. It's also correct on a subtextual level because if Bond really had such power, he'd have no need to challenge Daddy at all.

After Bond wins, Goldfinger must reestablish the balance of power by demonstrating that he too possesses a measure of Bond's sexual power, perfectly represented in his henchman Oddjob. Oddjob cuts off the head of a female statue, beautifully evoking what he did to Jill. And neither killing real women nor decapitating statues is a problem for the Goldfingers of the world, because they "own the club." Touché. Bond may have won the game, but he's still a youngster in Goldfinger's world.

Danger then arrives in the form of another woman. Tilly Masterson is a mystery to Bond, and Bond goes to great lengths to check her out. What's your last name? Where are you from? In other words, do you belong to *him*? What Bond discovers is she does, indirectly, belong to Goldfinger—because she is Jill's sister. Once this fact is revealed, Tilly is killed, again by Goldfinger's penis substitute (there, I said it), Oddjob. The boys all stop playing gunfight and rush to her side, where Bond seems truly traumatized. Again, his choice of the wrong woman has doomed her... and this time, he didn't even get to sleep with her. Castration? Well....

Do I need to go on about how the laser table is a castration device? There's nothing subtextual here—it's literal! Goldfinger is going right for the source of Bond's "power" just as Bond has gone for the source of his. And somehow this feels right. What's surprising about this scene is Bond does not escape. Goldfinger spares him. Goldfinger holds control the whole time, and it's Goldfinger who turns off the laser power. Bond's sexual power is now a gift from Daddy, and a conditional one at that.

Having made a deal with Daddy, the son awakes to find himself rewarded with what else but a prostitute. "My name is Pussy Galore." (If that's not the name of a prostitute, what is?) Again, Bond is very careful about ascertaining Pussy's sexual relationship with Goldfinger before he does anything. When Pussy tells him she's "Mr. Goldfinger's personal pilot," Bond asks, "Just how personal is that?" This question seems a little rude for an English gentleman until you understand the subtext at work here. After being made impotent by the laser-table deal, Bond needs to know whether Pussy is the ultimate insult or possible salvation for his sexual ego. Indeed, the filmmakers go out of their way to show us that Pussy is *not* Goldfinger's lover—just the opposite. Goldfinger wants her, but "no trespassing" is her motto. (In the book, Pussy is a lesbian; it's up to interpretation whether she is or isn't in the film. The "I'm immune" line is highly suggestive, as is her "flying circus" of fellow female "pilots.")

Once Bond establishes that Pussy isn't Goldfinger's sexual "employee," he pursues her aggressively. What better way to reclaim your manhood than by conquering a woman Daddy can't have? But Bond discovers getting your own woman is not as easy as stealing one that's already been broken in by Daddy. Here's where *Goldfinger* embraces its adolescence a little too closely. In the novel *The Spy Who Loved Me*, Fleming has the main character, Vivienne Michel, say, "All women secretly want to be raped." Unfortunately, *Goldfinger* offers up this as the logical solution to Bond's dilemma. Like it or not, Bond physically forces himself on Pussy in a way that he's never done in any film. But this act of violence does the trick, and Pussy is instantly converted. Even for a Bond film, this feels naïve. Nevertheless, the ritual is completed and allows Bond to engage in one last battle.

Having restored his sexual potency, Bond is ready to complete his mission. Tellingly, Bond's "conquest" of Pussy occurs after he has discovered the ultimate source of Goldfinger's power (an A-bomb). With Pussy as an ally, thwarting Daddy's latest "cheat" is not as impossible as first imagined. But Bond's final struggle is a physical one. He must battle the extension of Daddy's sexuality—namely, Oddjob. Bond does this by showing a superior understanding of the "source" of power as he literally overpowers Oddjob by electrocuting him. (It's interesting that the movie both opens and closes with Bond killing someone via electrocution.)

Having "killed off" Daddy's potency, Bond does not seem to sweat his final encounter with Goldfinger. Appropriately, Goldfinger is now costumed in a mock military uniform—a rather desperate attempt at masculine power—and is holding a gun that, with its gold plating, appears more feminine than powerful. The emasculated Goldfinger tells Bond that Miss Galore is "where she belongs—at the controls." Damn right she's at the controls! And those are Goldfinger's last words before he's sucked through the impossibly small space of the aircraft window in a sort of bizarre reverse-birth death. Goldfinger is more than dead. He's erased from existence.

"This is no time to be rescued," says Bond at the end of the film. That's right. Because having accomplishing his most important mission—liberating himself (albeit temporarily) from his own Oedipus Complex—Bond is free to enjoy the ultimate reward: pussy galore.

————————

JOHN COX was born and raised in Los Angeles, California, where he attended the USC School of Cinema-Television. John has worked as a professional screenwriter for the last ten years and has written projects for Warner Bros, DreamWorks, MGM, Sony, ABC, CBS, the USA Network, and more. John became a Bond fan when he saw his first and still favorite 007 film, *The Spy Who Loved Me*, in the summer of 1977. He collects James Bond first editions and is also an expert on the life of Harry Houdini. John lives in Hollywood, California.

"Bland...James Bland"

I N *GOLDENEYE*, JUDI DENCH'S M tells Bond he's a misogynist, sexist pig—a relic of the Cold War. Despite probably disqualifying Bond from being awarded the Employee of the Month parking space, the criticism was taken by 007 in characteristic stride. Bond had always had a prickly relationship with his previous onscreen bosses, but the scenario traditionally presented 007 and M more or less as unruly student and benevolent but stern headmaster. The *GoldenEye* exchange was the first attempt to shed some significant light on how Bond actually related to the figure of immediate authority in his otherwise freelance existence. As such, audiences were able to see human elements expressed that had not been explored in previous films. (The scene—and exchanges with M in future films of the Brosnan era—did take pains to note that there was an underlying mutual respect between the two.)

The aforementioned sequence was somewhat jarring for audiences because over the course of the previous thirty-two years, there were precious few attempts to explore the personal life or psyche of James Bond. Considering how intimately the public has come to know the films themselves, it is rather surprising how little they know about the central character of Agent 007. Ian Fleming's books were more generous with attempts to explain Bond's early life and some of his motivations, though even Bond's literary father seemed content to only offer the occasional tantalizing morsel of information. The films made Bond even more opaque—especially in contrast to other legendary screen heroes. You don't have to be a fanatic about the Superman movies to know Superman was born Kal-El on the planet Krypton and was sent to Earth as an infant before the doomed planet exploded. Likewise, it's virtually common knowledge that Bruce Wayne's Batman was ultimately motivated to fight crime because of the death of his parents at the hands of a mugger. However, the Bond films have always steered clear of providing in-depth background information about their central character—thus making Bond the cinematic equivalent of the man who hides in plain sight. He's the most visible presence in each film, but on the aggregate, the least interesting.

I've always been of the opinion that in a way Bond is one of the least important elements of his screen adventures. His primary focus is to serve as a catalyst for the actions of the far more interesting characters with whom he interacts. There is nothing intrinsically interesting about most of what we see Bond do. Yes, he gambles extensively on the inexplicably inexhaustible salary this British civil servant seems to have, and yes, he certainly dallies with the ready, willing, and able beauties he encounters at every turn. Beyond that, however, there is little evidence that Bond would even make an interesting dinner companion, let alone a larger-than-life figure. Indeed, the brief glimpse we're afforded of the first M's personal life (in *On Her Majesty's Secret Service*) shows him to be engrossed in the hobby of cataloging and displaying butterflies. While this may fall somewhere below attending a John Tesh concert in terms of cutting-edge behavior, it at least indicates that M has a passion for something tangible beyond the "sinful" excesses demonstrated by Bond. We certainly know Bond's interests don't extend to interior design. In the forty-plus years of the series, we're only invited into his London flat on two occasions. In *Dr. No* we find it to be tastefully but drably decorated, while in *Live and Let Die* the interior looks like a bad Peter Max painting and reminds one of why the '70s are referred to as the Decade that Style Forgot (let's not even mention that polyester safari suit Bond wore in *The Man With the Golden Gun*, with pockets that made him resemble Captain Kangaroo more than the top agent of MI6).

The lack of insight into Bond's past seems to be a consistent and deliberate strategy on the part of the filmmakers. Bond fans may consider it to be sacrilegious to accuse him of being bland, but any honest evaluation would force you to consider the following hypothetical question: Who would make a more interesting companion on a long airline flight,

Mr. Bond or Auric Goldfinger? The literary James Bond is a more complex character largely because the printed page allows the author to specify the character's emotions and mindset in great detail. The cinematic Bond is bound by the obvious restrictions imposed by celluloid: such aspects of his personality can only be hinted at without slowing the pace dramatically. Any attempt to provide an in-depth emotional analysis of Bond's psyche might inadvertently turn a 007 action epic into a Bergmanesque piece of pseudo-psychology. Because they have a more expansive canvas on which to present a character's background and emotional state, authors have the advantage over filmmakers. Thus, Ian Fleming and his successors John Gardner and Raymond Benson were able to flesh out the character much more fully.

Bond enthusiasts tend to pine away for the days when the films had not been carried away with an obsession with gadgetry and hardware, specifically the first two entries in the series, *Dr. No* and *From Russia With Love*. While those classics did indeed emphasize the more humanistic qualities of Bond's world, it would be an oversimplification to state that they included any serious attempts to give the character significant depth. Although these films are regarded as "serious" entries in the series, a close inspection of how Bond is presented proves that his characterization is equally opaque there as in later films. The introduction of hardware to the series began modestly with the famed lethal briefcase seen in *From Russia with Love*. When the Aston Martin DB5 became a cause célèbre in its own right in *Goldfinger*, the producers became obsessed with the notion of placing as much hardware around Bond as was humanly possible. A sly, self-effacing reference to this comes in *Thunderball* when Bond—fully loaded with a Sherman tank-size scuba jet pack on his back—is about to jump from a helicopter to join a raging battle beneath the sea. "…And the kitchen sink," he quips to Felix Leiter, who assures him, "On you, anything looks good!"

When producers Albert R. Broccoli and Harry Saltzman initially brought Bond to the screen, humor was not intended to be a main ingredient of the character. Although Fleming's books were considered to be "over the top" adventure stories, the literary Bond was not defined by his wit. As shooting on *Dr. No* got underway, the director Terence Young and star Sean Connery decided to inject some humor and wisecracks into the proceedings, as though giving the audience a wink and a nod that they were in on the absurdities of the plot. Fortuitously, they decided to play the humor in a straitlaced manner without overt reaction shots or moments of outright slapstick. It can be argued that the very first indication of Bond's wit comes in a rather non-descript sequence in *Dr. No*. En route to a meeting in Jamaica, Bond discovers his chauffeur is an enemy agent. After a brief struggle, the man commits suicide by biting into a cigarette laced with cyanide. Not wanting to be late for the appointment, Bond simply sits the hapless fellow upright in the back of the convertible and pulls up to the office where his meeting is being held. He casually comments to the security guard to "see to it that he doesn't get away" as the man does a double-take, seeing the corpse in the back seat. The sequence is modest in scope but set an important precedent for how we would come to perceive Bond. No one ever questions him about how the dead man ended up in his car, he doesn't even mention it in his meeting with government officials, and when the meeting ends he casually leaves the premises after getting the phone number of a sexy secretary—quite the contrast to those of us who can't even carry a nail clipper through airport security without incurring a body cavity search. Bond's ability to rise above mundane rules and regulations would become a mainstay of his character. Rules are for you and me, not for Mr. Kiss Kiss Bang Bang.

Both the gadgetry and the humor, while initially appealing innovations the series had made over the usual spy stories, quickly became the films' focus, upstaging the man who employed them. Sean Connery's desire to leave the franchise was exacerbated not only by his financial differences with producers Broccoli and Saltzman, but also by his increasing frustration with the character of Bond, who had by the late '60s been relegated to mostly pushing buttons to activate the latest hardware from Q Branch. Releasing Connery from his contract and hiring George Lazenby to succeed him in *On Her Majesty's Secret Service* provided a chance to do something different with Bond, and Peter Hunt, who had edited most of the previous films, was chosen to direct.

Hunt's vision represented the most dynamic attempt yet to flesh out the character of Bond and make him something more than a colorless hero around whom more exotic characters gravitated. He dispensed with the usual hardware and gave Bond only plausible, nonexotic gadgets that could be realistically woven into the story. Hunt and screenwriter Richard Maibaum were also determined to bring Bond as close to the roots of Fleming's vision as possible. The script followed Fleming's novel rather closely, with some exotic action sequences thrown in for cinematic effect.

Despite some rough edges due to inexperience, Lazenby acquitted himself well. While it would be a mistake to refer to his Bond as "warm and fuzzy," Maibaum's script did provide for ample sequences that allowed us to see a bit further into Bond's psychological makeup. When the film begins, Bond is still every bit the womanizer and perennial bachelor. His love affair with the equally adventurous and independent Contessa Tere-sa di Vincenzo allows him to find love for the first time, though he has to be initially prodded into dating her by her father, an organized crime boss who has promised to lead Bond to the elusive Blofeld if Bond "tames" his daughter's wild ways.

What begins as a business arrangement leads to a genuine love affair, and for the first time we get a depiction of Bond as a three-dimensional charac-ter—capable of tenderness, generosity, and ultimately heartbreak. The film depicts the couple's wedding, a sequence that also helps paint a more com-plete picture of Bond in subtle ways. (When he spies his emotionally dev-astated would-be lover Miss Moneypenny, tough guy Bond can't find the courage to actually address her in this awkward situation, but makes the sentimental gesture of silently tossing her his hat, knowing it will remain a treasured keepsake for her.) Bond's full emotional range is on view in the film's daring and tragic climax, where Tracy is murdered at the hands of Blofeld and his henchwoman Irma Bunt. The absence of a happy end-ing and the shattering final shot of Bond holding his beloved wife while he breaks down actually alienated some critics, who complained that 007 was now a mawkish figure. However, the ensuing years have been kind to the film, and Hunt's bold vision has now been acclaimed by many as a high-water mark of the series.

Conventional wisdom has said that if only Sean Connery had starred in *On Her Majesty's Secret Service*, it would have been a masterwork. The argument is an invalid one, however. By the time the film went into pro-duction, Connery's Bond had long ago segued into a flippant, rather emo-tionless character prone to making wisecracks and glossing over tragic events. It is highly doubtful that if Connery had starred in the film, the producers would have tampered with the formula in any substantial way. It is quite probable that *On Her Majesty's Secret Service* would have been just another Bond adventure, emphasizing technology over human emotion. (Indeed, the producers completely discarded the plot of the previous film, *You Only Live Twice*, and replaced the tale of a one-on-one struggle between Bond and Blofeld with an elaborate plot centering on rocket ships!)

Proof that the above stated theory is correct is borne out by the fact that Connery's return in *Diamonds Are Forever* in 1971 (replacing Lazenby, who quit after his one appearance as Bond) was a reversion to the old formula. In fact, this film is so over-the-top in terms of overt comedy that Connery's previous epics resemble arthouse films in comparison. The notion that this overt humor originated in the Roger Moore era that followed is contradict-ed by any objective analysis of *Diamonds Are Forever*.

The success of *Diamonds Are Forever* only *encouraged* the emphasis on humor during the Moore era. Much of this was in keeping with Moore's understandable desire to create Bond in his own mold—and by any definition he is a far more humorous person than his predecessor. However, a consequence of this formula was that even less attention was paid to fleshing out the character of Bond himself. Moore played Bond strictly tongue-in-cheek, with the quips flying as fast and frequently as the bullets. Although Moore is perfectly capable of giving a very good dramatic performance (*The Man Who Haunted Himself*, *The Wild Geese*, *Shout at the Devil*), he made it clear from day one that he felt the character of Bond was an absurdity in itself and played the role accordingly. He has frequently stated how ludicrous he thought it was to have a "secret agent" who is immediately identifiable the world over to the extent that bartenders recognize his drink preferences and casual acquaintances outside the intelligence industry are familiar with his name. (Witness diamond smuggler Tiffany Case's response to what she believes is the death of 007: "You just killed James Bond!"—as though she were discussing an iconic figure such as Walt Disney.)

By 1981, even Moore and the Bond producers realized that the character of Bond had been weakened to the point that he had become a bit of a bore. Even the blockbuster success of 1979's *Moonraker* could not hide the fact that the films had become almost exclusively about technology and slapstick comedy sequences. For the next film, *For Your Eyes Only*, producer Cubby Broccoli decided to bring the series "back to earth" both literally and figuratively. In doing so, there was a concerted attempt to humanize Bond, taking the emphasis off the flashier Bond trademarks and focusing on character development. In the pre-credits sequence we see him briefly in somber reflection at the grave of his late wife Tracy—a nice touch, and one of the few attempts to link any Bond actor with a previous Bond actor's films. Bond becomes involved with Melina, a young woman obsessed with avenging the murders of her parents, and shows a distinctly human side when he advises her about the emotional toll vengeance can take. *For Your Eyes Only* also took pains to revert the character to his earlier, hard-broiled persona, in one sequence shoving an enemy trapped in a car off a cliff and effectively reminding audiences that 007 had once been more than a stand-up comedian in a tuxedo.

Perhaps the most complex onscreen Bond persona was seen during the brief tenure of Timothy Dalton in *The Living Daylights* and *Licence to Kill*. Dalton is an intense actor who actually studied the works of Fleming in preparation for the role. In fact, certain silly sequences that had originally been planned for *Daylights* were eliminated because they would have been at odds with Dalton's determination to bring a more human element to the character. *Licence to Kill* comes the closest to giving significant background on Bond's psychological makeup. Instead of presenting us with a largely emotionless superman, the plot finds Bond acting in direct contrast to the philosophy he espouses in *For Your Eyes Only*, obsessed with tracking down the crime kingpin who has mutilated his friend Felix Leiter and murdered Leiter's new bride. For the first time, his relationship with M takes on a very meaningful dimension. Bond ignores M's orders to remove himself from his self-imposed mission of revenge and in doing so loses his license to kill. In fact, he becomes listed as a rogue agent. The film bristles with a realistic quality not seen in most previous Bonds, though audiences remain deeply divided about the end result. Some fans argue that the film is a refreshing digression from the spectacle and hardware associated with the series, while others feel the movie more resembles *Miami Vice* than vintage 007. Indisputably, however, Dalton largely succeeded in his quest to make Bond a more comprehensive and complex character. Where Moore's Bond gave only window dressing and cursory attempts to flesh out the character, Dalton made a daring and overt attempt to inject considerable humanity into 007's persona.

When Pierce Brosnan replaced Timothy Dalton, he brought an exuberance and sense of fun to the part that had been missing for many years, but also attempted to continue Dalton's tradition of making Bond a more nuanced, less mechanized character. His attempts to inject humor were more successful than his predecessor's uncomfortable attempts at making quips; Brosnan's Bond was a letter-perfect hybrid of his predecessor's strengths and his own personal touches.

Critics and sociologists have long pondered the reasons for James Bond's lasting popularity. In one of the Sherlock Holmes films, Basil Rathbone affectionately describes his colleague Dr. Watson as the one fixed point in an ever-changing world. The same backhanded compliment helps explain the durability of the Bond films. Although society and the world have changed dramatically since 1962, Bond has endured. It may very well be that Bond's blandness is the reason. The minimal background and character development Bond has been given makes him capable of being adapted to the needs of any audience.

When the series returned in 1995 with Brosnan in *GoldenEye*, there was much speculation that Bond was about as relevant in the 1990s as the Bay City Rollers and Nehru jackets. Since Dalton's last film, the Cold War had ended and the Soviet Union had collapsed. The smart money said that

ASK DR. YES

Dear Dr. Yes,

I also used to work for SPECTRE, but after I made love to James I came to realize that a life of crime was wrong. He's a wonderful man—and the sex is great—but whenever someone shoots at him he keeps using me as a human shield. I'm starting to worry that this means he doesn't take our relationship seriously. What should I do?

Help me,
Nervous in New Orleans

Dear Nervous,

Don't be silly! James would never use you as a human shield unless:

 a) *he believed you were working with the enemy,*
 b) *you were atrocious in bed, or*
 c) *a bullet was coming at him and you were the only thing handy.*

Have you considered being more giving, sexually? This isn't all about your needs. In the meantime, I'll be taking out a life insurance policy in your name, proceeds to go to the 007 Champagne Fund (Dom Perignon is not cheap, particularly the earlier vintages). Good luck!

Bond was irrelevant in the new world order, but the producers felt otherwise, and they addressed the lingering rumors that the character was out of place in the 1990s by updating the attitude of Brosnan's Bond toward the third long-standing hallmark of the Bond franchise: women.

The most defining aspect of Bond's lifestyle may be his relationship with women, though with the exception of the Lazenby film, his lovers have been sexual conquests rather than emotional relationships. Although generally regarded as a "love-'em-and-leave-'em" playboy, Bond's apologists can make the case that he does not manipulate naïve women; they use him for their selfish pleasure as much as he uses them for his, and the women he's been involved with have largely been the ultimate symbols of female liberation: highly intelligent, highly capable, and very courageous. But in general, Bond's relationships with women have remained fairly consistent throughout the films. He is not immune to falling in love, but he shows little willpower in rejecting the advances of the opposite sex, and the consequences (to him, if not to his female partner) are few. It wasn't until the Dalton era that Bond was presented in a more mature light in terms of sexual practices. With the exception of one pre-credits sequence dalliance, Dalton's Bond remains monogamous in *The Living Daylights* and keeps his sexual activities all in the line of duty in *Licence to Kill*.

Brosnan's Bond is refreshingly complex and "modern" in his dealings with women. Like his predecessors, he has plenty of dalliances with minor female characters (there must be a bus carrying "roadies" for sexy secret agents), but his Bond is more prone to romance than sex. In *Tomorrow Never Dies* he becomes literally depressed when confronted with a previous lover, Paris Carver, for whom he has been carrying a torch. Her death leaves him quite shaken—an emotion generally downplayed in the previous eras, when Bond would gloss over the death of a lover or colleague (*On Her Majesty's Secret Service* and *Licence to Kill* being the main exceptions).

But could the character's evolution go so far as to render him entirely unrecognizable? Bond's use of violence has shocked audiences since 1962 when, in *Dr. No*, Bond shoots the villainous Prof. Dent even though the man's gun is empty of bullets. A cinematic hero killing someone unnecessarily when the other man is defenseless was considered to be so provocative that the censors forced the producers to eliminate several of the final shots Bond fires into Dent's prone body. Similarly, Brosnan's Bond needlessly kills the beautiful but treacherous Elektra King in *The World Is Not Enough*. But while times had changed enough that the sequence, which would have been unthinkable in an earlier era, did not produce much controversy, it seems out of place with the generally chivalrous nature of agent 007. It's one thing to kill an unarmed man, but extending that practice to *women* feels out of touch with what has been clearly established of Bond's persona.

It is likely that the character will continue to evolve, and it may be that decades from now audiences will embrace a very different agent 007 then we have known. Indeed, as this is written, Daniel Craig has yet to bring his own version to an eagerly awaiting fan base. As society's values change, concessions will always be made to the character to keep him in tune with modern audiences, but one hopes the producers continue their practice of not making the changes *too* drastic in order to maintain relevancy with the youth market—or I fear one day we may actually see a marquee that boasts the dreaded words: "Ludacris *IS* James Bond!"

LEE PFEIFFER is the author/co-author of numerous books about the cinema and is regarded as one of the foremost James Bond scholars. His book *The Essential Bond: An Authorized Guide to the World of 007* (written with Dave Worrall) is the top-selling Bond film book of all time. Pfeiffer is also the editor-in-chief of Cinema Retro magazine, dedicated to films of the 1960s and 1970s (www.cinemaretro.com). He resides in New Jersey.

MARK W. TIEDEMANN

The Spy
Who Would Not Die
An Alternate History of Bond

"**N**AME'S BOND. JAMES BOND."
With those words, the moviegoing world was first introduced to Ian Fleming's potentially explosive character in the first major motion picture production of *Dr. No* in 1963. What followed has frustrated and delighted Bond fans for years. The path by which James Bond finally became the iconic cinematic figure he is today took numerous unexpected turns and, by some opinions, far too long to attain prominence. What should have been the start of a phenomenon stubbornly refused to live up to box office expectations that, after the first three films, cast the franchise into the ranks of made and remade, attempted and reattempted, taking years before the right combination finally produced a lasting success.

What makes one film a box office phenomenon and another, well, not? Hollywood and its various clones have puzzled over this question since D. W. Griffith railed against the studios for hacking to pieces his arguably superb masterworks. One ingredient which all name and then fail to define in any useful terms is Chemistry. A film has it or it doesn't. The frustrating part is that no one knows which it is until the product is finished and on-screen and the viewing public either loves it...or doesn't.

When Ian Fleming's hero attracted the interest of Harry Saltzman and

Albert Broccoli, everything ought to have fallen into place. The pair had formed EON Productions with the expectation of producing top-flight films, starting with—they hoped—the James Bond franchise. Fleming believed he had found the right backing. Since his frustrating attempts at gaining an American company's interest—after the mixed results of the television production of *Casino Royale*—Fleming was delighted by both the British sensibilities and the grandiosity of EON thinking toward the project. Broccoli especially possessed a keen sense of marketing and had drawn up an elaborate campaign to prepare the public to receive this new kind of hero.

As months dragged on in the search for the right Bond, though, enthusiasm suffered. What Fleming wanted ran slightly at odds with the motion picture realities Saltzman and Broccoli understood so well. Actor after actor tested, interviewed, read, only to be rejected for the most obscure reasons, mainly to do with Fleming's idea of what Bond ought to look like, sound like, move like. He was the creator, after all, and intended to have considerable input in the making of the films, something both Saltzman and Broccoli had agreed to but now viewed with growing reluctance.

Finally, with the acceptance of Scottish actor Sean Connery, it looked like things were going forward.

Connery broke an ankle on the second day of production. Complications mounted and Saltzman argued that it would be better to put off shooting until Connery was healed. Other disputes had time to emerge and before production could resume, Connery left the project. (He later took Richard Burton's place as King Arthur in the stage production of Lerner and Lowe's *Camelot* and, eventually, starred in the film version as well.)

Another round of interviews commenced. Among those discarded: Patrick McGoohan, Ian Hendry, Peter O'Toole, Anthony Quayle, Rod Taylor, Ken Adams, Tony Franciosa. (Ironically, given his later contribution to the Bond canon, Richard Burton did not even audition.) Fleming, impatient with the process and needing to begin work on a new novel, withdrew, trusting EON to make the right decision. At this point, several factors converged.

The popularity of the Bond novels had soared when President John F. Kennedy mentioned how much he liked them in an interview. Kennedy's friend and supporter Frank Sinatra had looked into obtaining the rights to the books for his own production company. Failing that, he sought to have some involvement, and it was because of his recommendation that Saltzman and Broccoli interviewed, tested, and hired Lawrence Harvey to play Bond.

While at first glance this may have seemed a perfectly reasonable choice, Fleming was furious. He had needed convincing to hire Connery because he had felt the Scottsman too handsome. To Fleming, Bond needed to look hard and experienced. The trick was to balance that harsh look with the obvious sensuality the character exuded. Harvey, compared to Connery, lacked whatever "toughness" Connery brought to the character, but he certainly possessed the urbanity and confidence for the part.

Pacified by these arguments, Fleming stepped back and let EON do its job.

Dr. No, after several months' delay, finally went into production. Joseph Wiseman had remained with the project as Dr. No, but others had been replaced. Jack Lord had to leave the project to work on his own television series, *Stoney Burke*, which aired in 1962. Burt Reynolds stepped in to play the part of CIA agent Felix Leiter. Actress Senta Berger was cast as Honey Ryder, and thanks to the remarkable talents of several other excellent character actors, confidence in the film ran high.

Its release during the Christmas season of 1963 proved unfortunate. Factors no one could have predicted conspired to weaken the response it might have gotten even six months earlier. Two in particular seem relevant to the subsequent history of the franchise. The assassination of President Kennedy had shaken the United States and, indeed, much of the world. People were somber. The Cold War did not seem fit subject matter now for the antics of a secret agent of such unlikely qualities. As well, Lawrence Harvey's previous role as a programmed assassin in the Sinatra vehicle *The Manchurian Candidate* returned to haunt him in this incarnation. People seemed unwilling to accept him as James Bond.

Still, the film received decent reviews, and the box office was not so bad as to discourage EON entirely, so plans went forward for the next picture.

From Russia With Love was, by all accounts, a better film. Better scripted, it also adhered more closely to the novel. Harvey seemed more at home in the character and the setting. Production suffered few mishaps and the schedule was met. Box office turned out a little better.

But there were problems. The chemistry between Harvey and Lois Maxwell, who played Moneypenny, was not up to expectations. Rumors of animosity on the set seemed substantiated when she was replaced by model-turned-actress Charlotte Rampling. By the time *Goldfinger* was finished, Saltzman's other franchise—the Harry Palmer films—was underway and doing well at the box office. Michael Caine's dry, working-class spy caught the public imagination and the films' popularity suggested they had the potential everyone had hoped for from Bond. *Goldfinger* did less than the previous two films and, with Fleming's unfortunate death in 1964, EON lost interest in the franchise.

Ordinarily, the story might have ended there, except for the ineluctible attractiveness of the James Bond character. The books continued to do well, even after Fleming's death, and arrangements were underway to franchise the character and find new writers. The groundswell of popularity brought the films back as arthouse favorites until, inevitably, a new film was announced in 1968. The new production company, headed by Martin Ritt (*The Spy Who Came In From The Cold, Hud, The Outrage*), bought rights to one novel from the Fleming Estate—*On Her Majesty's Secret Service*. By the bizarre currents of the film industry, Sean Connery was once more tapped to play the spy, and this time nothing went wrong. A number of the cast from the first films returned, including Lois Maxwell as Moneypenny and Bernard Lee as M. With Diana Rigg playing the one true love of Bond's life, the film did moderately well. Connery left immediately, though, to begin filming the movie version of *Camelot* (he would work with Ritt again on *The Molly Maguires*), and *On Her Majesty's Secret Service* turned out to be a one-off hit. Critics waxed nostalgic on the possibilities for the franchise had Connery been able to make the first three. Ritt made plans for a second film and actor Albert Finney was contracted to step in as 007. However, as with so many Hollywood projects that are picked up and inexplicably dropped, *Live and Let Die* never began shooting.

In retrospect, it's been generally agreed that too-early success of the films might have led to an inevitable excess of cinematic device, dragging the character further and further away from the fine execution of the novels. While the big-screen possibilities in Fleming's stories are certainly present, James Bond remained throughout the series a study in character under stress. The strength of the written oeuvre is the almost claustrophobic intimacy achieved by putting the reader inside the head of a man who lives dangerously in service to his country and a set of principles which, while sometimes difficult to define, remain solid. Big explosions, hair-raising chases, shoot-outs, and spectacular fight scenes—which are the basic lexicon of the so-called Blockbuster—can and often do overshadow the subtler and worthier elements of story. (The assault on Blofeld's mountain retreat in the Connery film is a good example.)

Because of the growing popularity of the four films and the continued success of the novels into the '70s, inevitably other projects were launched, most never to be completed. American television producer Bruce Geller secured rights to do a pilot for a series based on Bond (something Fleming had wanted to do back in the '50s). The pilot was produced, but Geller had changed some of the dynamics. A bemused Roger Moore played Bond opposite a far more involved Moneypenny sharply played by Julie London. They appeared more as a team, with Moneypenny actually working in the field, and the implication of an ongoing liaison between them curiously "domesticated" Bond. The show was not picked up, leaving this oddity for the hardcore buffs.

More significantly, Solar Productions—actor Steve McQueen's company—optioned *Diamonds Are Forever*. Director Philip D'Antoni (*The Seven-Ups, The French Connection*) was tagged to direct and Michael York chosen to play Bond. Other cast members for this outing hint at the possibilities: Claire Bloom as Moneypenny and George C. Scott as M. Testing was done and a few scenes shot entirely, but the project was abandoned after encountering a host of technical difficulties on set.

The option—including both D'Antoni and actress Katherine Ross as Tiffany Case—passed to Malpaso Productions. Clint Eastwood was rumored to have wanted to play the part of Bond himself, which would have made him the second American to do so, but it never got out of pre-production.

The flurry of activity over the various novels died down after that. The James Bond franchise seemed about to enter a flat period. Sales had tapered off, despite the appearance of a new novel penned by Anthony Burgess. The nearly four hundred pages of *The Parsifal Dossier* dwarfed previous Bond novels and almost single-handedly lifted Bond into the realms of the literary. To this day, however, of all the Bond stories, it remains unoptioned, despite having been number one on the *Times* list for nearly nine weeks. (Burgess even discussed the notion with Stanley Kubrick, who seemed briefly interested in the idea, having never done an espionage film.)

All of which brings us finally to the Granada Television Productions series, beginning in 1978 with Sam Neill as Bond and Lynn Redgrave as Moneypenny. In a rare concession to television, Richard Burton was convinced to play M. Other notables in the cast included Derek Jacobi as Q and Linda Thorson as Sylvia Trench.

Its success in America and the popularity of British shows like *I, Claudius* and *Upstairs, Downstairs* suggested that the time was right for a first-rate thriller series. In the past, there had been several solid British spy shows, like *Danger Man* and its curious spin-off *The Prisoner*, as well as less serious programs like *The Avengers*, which had proved very popular in the United States.

The production benefited from the smaller format and its more modest demands. Troy Kennedy-Martin's scripts hued tightly to the novels, and the two- and three-part presentations allowed full examination of the details of Fleming's creations. Also, the episodes followed the books chronologically, beginning with *Casino Royale* and proceeding through, even as far as placing the short stories in context within the series. Development of the character became possible and, indeed, central to Sam Neill's performance.

"It was really the scriptwriting that made it," Neill recalled in an interview. "That and the genuine love of the material. All of us had been fans for years."

An important decision early on was to leave the stories set in their time, the late '50s and early '60s.

"Bond transcends time to some extent," director Martin Campbell explained, "but the background is all important. The Cold War, of which Bond is a creature, has gone through definite phases. Fleming wrote about the post-Stalinist period, which with the birth of the Space Race became a curiously romantic time for some people. Technology was beginning to come into its own as an element of story, but it was also and more importantly when style began to matter. Take, for instance, that marvelous opening sequence in Harry Saltzman's *Funeral In Berlin* film, where you see the stark contrast between East and West Berlin. In a very real sense, that's where the Cold War was fought, and Fleming had a grasp of that. That's why Bond is as much cultural icon as spy."

Filmed on location whenever possible, the production took advantage of Jamaica, Munich, and Singapore, as well as the facilities of England's famous Shepherton Studios.

The villains marched through played admirably by a series of excellent actors, including Leo McKern as Drax, John Rhys-Davies as Goldfinger, David Souchet as Dr. No, and an early appearance by Russell Crowe as Grant, the assassin.

The production values of the series lent a seriousness to the Bond stories that, as discussed, might easily have been lost with early success in the theatrical film versions. Neill's Bond remains plausible throughout—tough, smart, and humanly vulnerable. By the end of the run, the international cult following had reinvigorated the franchise and more films went into production over the next ten years. Sam Neill reprised the role once on the big screen, in a Steven Spielberg production of *Moonraker*.

Popularity began to surge. In a rush to get the newest take on Bond into theaters, filmmakers crowded through the door opened by the Neill series. Spielberg's attempt to buy up all the rights to the franchise failed, although he managed to obtain exclusive ownership of *Thunderball*. Subsequently, no new version of that novel has ever been made.

In 1983, six new productions were underway, ranging from the pedestrian-though-violent (Arthur Hill's body-strewn *Octopussy*) to the genuinely macabre (Wes Craven's supernatural take on *Live And Let Die*) to the bizarre (Alec Baldwin's performance in the Blake Edwards production of *Goldfinger*, which could never seem to decide whether to be funny or serious).

Most notable was the first X-rated version. Just Jaeckin, the French producer/director (*Emmanuelle*), cast Sylvia Kristel as the mysterious woman in *The Spy Who Loved Me* opposite Nicholas Clay, who managed the remarkable feat of maintaining a Bond-like poise and tasteful cool while being in the nude through nearly a third of the screen time. The dreamlike quality Jaeckin achieved took the film far from the source material, and Kristel seems alternately to be a Russian spy, Moneypenny, and Sylvia Trench, though she is ultimately a Mata Hari figure. It is also remarkable for Bond films in that no one dies.

The Spy Who Loved Me served more as a model to be reacted against rather than anything to follow, and the next film had strikingly little romance, not to mention a total lack of sex, despite starring Mel Gibson as Bond opposite Kim Basinger in John McTiernan's *Diamonds Are Forever*. McTiernan gave the film intensity, but stuck to the espionage throughout. Rumors of love scenes on the cutting room floor have circulated for years, but the icy professionalism displayed in Gibson's Bond seems to preclude a softer side, despite Ms. Basinger's allure as Tiffany Case. Anthony Hopkins is admirable as M, but there is no Moneypenny and, even more remarkably, no Q.

The unremitting seriousness of the McTiernan film is completely offset by the lunacy of *Boldfinger* with John Cleese as Bond and Tracey Ulman as Moneypenny. The screenplay, penned by Cleese and other Monty Python alumni Palin and Idle, took segments from a number of novels and combined them in a pastiche. Unexpectedly, a lawsuit from the owners of *Thunderball* attempted to block release of the film, arguing that the underwater sequences came from that novel. Attorneys for the production company successfully refuted the claim, demonstrating that the sequence in question was originally in a Jules Verne novel, and in any event ownership of one novel did not grant copyright of the entire ocean as backdrop for fiction.

Among the oddest film versions to emerge from this period is Roman Polanski's film of *The Hildebrand Rarity*, which cast Liam Neeson as a somber, almost morose James Bond. Among the bleaker portrayals, it is perhaps an appropriate coda to the Cold War, which would come to an official end not two years after the film's release.

Odder still, however, was the Andrew Lloyd Weber musical *BOND*, which premiered in London, starring pop star George Michael as the eponymous secret agent and Madonna as Moneypenny. The villain, though called "Mr. E," is a thinly veiled Goldfinger, surprisingly well done by the American singer Meatloaf.

As the Bond Legacy entered the '90s, small studio productions of the various novels and short stories popped up like mushrooms after rain. A host of production companies, directors, and actors filed through the Bond turnstile, handing out more and more outré interpretations. The nostalgia for the Cold War, perverse as it seemed, offered a fertile period for the last of the superspies. The wear and tear on the originals began to show by the turn of the century, and if new Bond adventures were to be filmed they would necessarily have to be based on new material.

The Estate had licensed the right to do new stories and novels to a number of writers over the years. Playboy Magazine continued to publish a number of them, having early on become identified with the secret agent. But the filmmakers stuck to their own visions rather than adapt these new literary entries, with mixed results.

Through the '80s and '90s, though, the Sam Neill Bonds have remained a hallmark.

"It's not a question of style over substance," scenarist Kennedy-Martin noted. "God knows, some of the movies have more style than we could have afforded! No, it's style *and* substance, working together at each other's level. Which I suppose is another way of saying, it's a matter of character placed effectively in context. Chemistry, I suppose."

Chemistry was the one element overwhelmingly present in the 1997 Spike Lee production starring Denzel Washington and Sharon Stone. Despite the skepticism of the critics, *Over the Edge*, in its depiction of Bond as an agent assigned the assassination of a high-level operative in the Middle East, displayed a level of political savvy and tension straight out of the novels.

As the twenty-first century begins, new Bond projects loom on the horizon. This past year Pixar released its completely CGI version, *007*, featuring the voice talents of Hugh Grant, Catherine Zeta-Jones, Mike Myers, and Dennis Franz. The computer animation was superb, but the production is remarkable also for being the first R-rated animated feature film since Ralph Bakshi's *Cool World*.

Also among those most eagerly anticipated is the Tim Burton production. The details have been kept under tightest security; the only thing known about it with any certainty is that Sean Connery will return, this time in the role of M, although the "top contenders for the lead" rumor names Tom Cruise, Ralph Fiennes, and Al Pacino. Connery, however, refuses to comment.

"I nearly launched the whole thing," Sir Sean said, "just as my career was taking off. Now it may be one of my last projects."

In fact, Bond is likely to outlive him. Over the past four and half decades the secret agent has built up a huge fan base. From uncertain beginnings into an uncertain era, James Bond may yet find it possible to save the world.

———

MARK W. TIEDEMANN is the author of *Mirage* and *Chimera*, both in the Asimov's Robot Mystery series; *Compass Reach* (part of the Secantis Sequence), for which he earned a nomination for the Philip K. Dick Award; and *Remains*. He has also contributed to the Smart Pop book *The Anthology at the End of the Universe*.

Drink Like Bond

ANDREA CARLO CAPPI

BOND IS, OF COURSE, a man who likes his drinks. In the novel *Casino Royale* he declares Tattinger the best champagne, while in Fleming's *Moonraker* his preferred vodka is Wolfschmidt from Riga (not easy to find). Drinks in the movies often depended on locations and sponsors. And of course the movie Bond is addicted to vodka martinis. But there are different literary Bond cocktails that might be sipped by a would-be Bond.

Classic Bond Drinks

Americano
007 enjoys it in Fleming's novels *Casino Royale, From Russia with Love*, and short stories "From a View to a Kill" and "Risico." His personal recipe: Bitter Campari, Cinzano vermouth, lemon peel, and Perrier water.

Dry Martini
One of Bond's (and his author's) favorite cocktails. He drinks it in Fleming's novels *Live and Let Die, Thunderball*, and *Diamonds Are Forever*, and anticipates it in the short story "007 in New York." It's supposed to be about 6/7 London dry gin and 1/7 vermouth (possibly Italian, possibily Martini, but Bond drinks it also with American-made vermouth), with olives or a lemon twist (my personal suggestion).

Negroni

One of my personal favorites. Drunk by Bond in Fleming's short story "Risico," it's made with London dry gin, Bitter Campari, and red vermouth, decorated with half an orange slice. Only side effect: by the time you really start enjoying it, the glass is empty and you have to order a second one.

The Vesper

Bond's personal creation in the novel *Casino Royale*. 3/4 London dry gin, 1/4 vodka, a bit of Kina Lillet (very hard to find nowadays), and lemon peel, served in a champagne goblet. Not intended to support long-lasting relationships.

Vodka Martini

Just like the dry martini recipe, but with vodka instead of gin—and, of course, shaken, not stirred, as most Bond movies remind us. The only exception is in *You Only Live Twice*, where Charles Gray offers it stirred, not shaken. In the novels it appears in *Moonraker, Diamonds Are Forever*, and *Dr. No*. In the film version of the latter, Sean Connery has a medium dry martini (half vodka, half vermouth).

More Martini Recipes for Would-Be Bonds

I like to think that Bond would just get bored drinking the same vodka martini, shaken not stirred. Today, in Italy but also in several countries in the world, there are some "Bond Point" bars (from London to Athens to Hong Kong) offering a huge variety of drinks and cocktails from 007 novels and films. Bartender Luca Coslovich from Milan's Palace Hotel (where Bond went in John Gardner's novel *Never Send Flowers*) even created his own variation, a Gold Vodka Martini, which deserves to be tried at least once in your life. The recipe is secret, but one of its ingredients is actually gold.

Here are my few humble martini suggestions.

Suicide Special

Three parts vodka (original Russian grain vodka if possible), three parts London dry gin, one part Martini extra-dry vermouth, and three drops of lemon juice; shake with ice and serve.

Spanish Martini

Six parts Larios dry gin (from Spain), one part Martini extra-dry vermouth;

shake or stir with ice, and add a lemon twist. (I'm not sponsored by Larios, but I should be, after drinking the stuff for all these years!)

Convective Vodka Martini

No shaker around? Don't worry. Put in your martini glass a few drops of lemon and a very little bit of room-temperature Martini extra-dry vermouth (or white vermouth, if you want a slightly sweeter touch); then add, generously, your favorite ice-cold Russian vodka. The laws of physics will be on your side: through convective streams inside the glass, the warmer vermouth and lemon juice molecules will mix perfectly with the cold vodka molecules and you'll have a wonderful "natural" martini. (That's all I got from all my years at the university, apart from the know-how required to correctly translate the nuclear bomb scenes in Bond books.)

THE
JAMES BOND
DEBATES

RAY DEMPSEY

What Is the Best Bond Movie?

🔫

Bonding...
by the Numbers

O N AN EARLY JAMES Bond site, alt.jamesbond, the easiest way to initiate a good argument was to state categorically that (pick a title) was the *best* Bond movie. There wasn't a movie, no matter how awful, that wasn't defended with vigor as being the best; however, without some benchmark of drama like Aristotle's *Theory of Tragedy*, picking the best Bond movie is like picking the best color, the best greeting card, or the best wedding gown. It's entirely subjective and therefore hard to defend.

That said, there are elements in all the Bond films that sparkle like little diamonds. When a defender talks about one film being the best, it is often because of one of these factors. Perhaps he or she loves the excitement of the prologue, or the intricacy of the plot. Perhaps a spectacular villain or a glamorous Bond girl makes that film his or her favorite. Perhaps the special effects, the cars, the location, or even the music propelled it to preferred status. So, in order to determine precisely which Bond film is, in fact, the best, I will be examining what each of these elements contributes to the whole, reviewing the films and, with tongue firmly in cheek, assigning a value to each of the parts, in hopes of coming up with a somewhat more objective, by-the-numbers winner—and ending those online squabbles once and for all.[1]

---

[1] The actor playing Bond is a major element in any Bond film, but rating them requires more than a short discussion of Connery's toughness, Lazenby's looks, Moore's humor, Dalton's intensity, or Brosnan's charm.

Before looking at the works produced by EON, we'll use a film that fell outside of the Bond franchise as an example of how the process of assigning points will work. There were several attempts at Bond other than EON's productions. Fleming's early sale of the *Casino Royale* screen rights spawned an episode of a live broadcast called "Climax!" in the early days of black-and-white TV, starring Barry Nelson as an American Jimmy (!) Bond with sidekick Felix Leiter and a spoof starring Peter Sellers and Woody Allen, an off-the-wall comedy that bore no resemblance to Fleming's story. The most successful of the spin-offs was *Never Say Never Again* based on the same story line as *Thunderball*.

Never Say Never Again didn't incorporate the standard "Bond Film" elements, but it was a serious and, in some camps, quality production. It starred Sean Connery looking better than he did in *Diamonds Are Forever* and featured one of the loopiest Bond villains, Fatima Blush, played by Barbara Carrera. The cast included other superb personnel, including Klaus Maria Brandauer (equally loopy!), and Kim Basinger.

NEVER SAY NEVER AGAIN		
Prologue:	0/5	(since there was no prologue)
Plot:	20/30	(unoriginal, based on *Thunderball*)
Villains:	16/15	(Ms. Blush, surely worth the extra point!)
Bond Girls:	5/15	
FX:	15/20	(nice tango by 007 and Miss Basinger)
Cars:	5/10	(no cars, but an exciting motorcycle incident)
Music:	0/5	
# of Major Locations:	7	(bonus points)
Total: 68 of 100 points		

Got the idea? Then let's get started.

Moonraker

Moonraker often snags the prize for last place. I won't argue. Although some of the space scene special effects are impressive, the plot and Jaws are over the top and the key heavy, Hugo Drax, is a bore. (In the novel *Moonraker* he was in danger of killing 007 with boredom with his long-winded life story and why he intends to use *Moonraker* to kill a few million people, a far more modest proposal than his movie alter ego's plan of wiping out the Earth's population.) Dr. Holly Goodhead (Lois Chiles) makes a gorgeous Bond girl and is the high point of the film.

MOONRAKER		
Prologue:	5/5	
Plot:	0/30	
Villains:	-5/15	(for Drax's sleeping pill villainy)
Bond Girls:	15/15	
FX:	18/20	(impressive space battle)
Cars:	0/10	
Music:	5/5	
# of Major Locations:	8	
Total: 46 of 100 points		

The Man with the Golden Gun

Call them clever, grandiose, impossible, or downright nutty, the twists of the plots keep us interested, if sometimes puzzled. (Why destroy the world to control it?) Here, using the Solex Agitator would give *The Man with the Golden Gun* the power of the sun. Actress Maud Adams is this story's Bond girl. But aside from her, the story didn't offer much to recommend it other than the clever use of cars: it converted the AMC Matador into an airplane, and in a spectacular scene had a car shoot up a twisted ramp, part of a destroyed bridge, and complete a 360 degree roll to land upright on the other side of a river!

THE MAN WITH THE GOLDEN GUN		
Prologue:	0/5	(too comical considering the deadly purpose)
Plot:	10/30	
Villains:	10/15	
Bond Girls:	10/15	
FX:	12/20	(the 360-degree roll and the airplane conversion)
Cars:	-2/10	(using the Matador in the first place)
Music:	4/5	
# of Major Locations:	6	
Total: 50 of 100 points		

A View to a Kill

Discussions involving 007 inevitably mention whether the action is plausible or ridiculous. *A View to a Kill* opens with an action that would probably be considered impossible but actually was accomplished by stuntman B. J. Worth: the parachute leap from the Eiffel Tower. The only thing that mars the sequence is the chase scene that follows with Bond driving a Renault taxi that has been cut in half in an accident. Compared with gassing everyone in the world as in *Moonraker*, scoundrel Max Zorin's plan to flood Silicon Valley by causing an earthquake so his business could control the microchip market almost makes sense. Q supplies Bond with a few useful devices including a minicopier to duplicate a check for evidence, a pen microchip tracking device, and a camera ring. And while it wasn't a Q device, Zorin's conversion of a construction shed into a blimp was pretty spiffy.

A VIEW TO A KILL		
Prologue:	5/5	(the tower jump)
Plot:	5/30	
Villains:	5/15	(all 5 for Grace, yet she turns out to be a good guy!)
Bond Girls:	10/15	(pretty, but screams more than Fay Wray)
FX:	19/20	
Cars:	0/10	
Music:	4/5	
# of Major Locations:	6	
Total: 54 of 100 points		

The Living Daylights

In *The Living Daylights*, we meet a new James Bond, Timothy Dalton, a 007 who didn't crank up the hearts of many critics or followers. However, I thought his rather serious (almost dour) portrayal was more in line with the character that Ian Fleming had in mind. Unfortunately, the story line was weak and MI6 must have told Q to empty the warehouse of every gimmick they had to make up for it. There were three nice touches: the Aston Martin Volante; Kara Milovy, the Czech cellist, played by Maryam d'Abo; and the campy downhill escape on the cello case.

THE LIVING DAYLIGHTS		
Prologue:	5/5	(a nice training assault on Gibraltar)
Plot:	5/30	
Villains:	2/15	(bland compared with other Bond foes)
Bond Girls:	15/15	(how can you not love a cellist?)
FX:	19/20	
Cars:	5/10	
Music:	4/5	
# of Major Locations:	7	
Total: 62 of 100 Points		

Dr. No

Dr. No, the first of the EON franchise, predates the signature gun-barrel theme but opens well with its quirky "Three Blind Mice" motif and the killing of a British agent in Jamaica, followed by the famous introduction by Sean Connery, "Bond, James Bond." One of the virtues of *Dr. No* for Ian Fleming admirers is that it stuck fairly close to the novel's plot; however, in the book he agonizes over having to kill as part of his 007 rating while in the film he knows that Professor Dent has an unloaded gun and deliberately kills him and intentionally pumps a couple more bullets into his body.

An element in *Dr. No* later developed more fully was the wisecrack remark (some say overly developed in Roger Moore films). Another was its use of a marvelous villain. Dr. No is played chillingly by Joseph Wiseman, whose hooded eyes look through, not at, his enemies. And when Ursula Andress walked out of the sea, she initiated the parade of lovely women who later played Bond's lovers, foils, and hopeful assassins. Although it had not yet fully developed what would become Bond trademarks, *Dr. No* still earns a respectable score.

DR. NO		
Prologue:	0/5	(didn't exist)
Plot:	20/30	
Villains:	15/15	
Bond Girls:	15/15	
FX:	5/20	(the cardboard "dragon")
Cars:	2/10	(not a DB5, but that sweet little Sunbeam Alpine deserves something)
Music:	5/5	
# of Major Locations:	2	
Total: 64 of 100 points		

Octopussy

Power-crazed Kamal Khan, in league with a genuine screwball Russian general, Orlov, is the antagonist in *Octopussy*. Their plot was to steal an atomic bomb and set it off on an American base in Germany so that European anger would drive the Americans out and allow the Russians to invade Western Europe. Maud Adams starred as Octopussy, the leader of a traveling circus, a cult figure...and a gem smuggler. Khan and General Orlov used her to smuggle the bomb onto the base. The film is rife with gorgeous Octopussy girls, weird villains, and spectacular Indian locations. Of all the deadly weapons used in the Bond films, I have to tip my hat to the spin-saw, a circular saw on a yo-yo line that descends to slice up people who have offended Mr. Kahn. An early high point in the story was Bond's use of a small jet plane to escape from a Cuban-like military base. The AcroStar is engaged in flight by missiles and Bond escapes by flying through the rapidly closing doors of a hanger; the pursuing missile smashes into the closed door, blowing the building to pieces. Oh, yes, and Q provides a video-screen watch for Bond. Lacking a good song named "Octopussy," the company had the good sense to have Rita Coolidge sing "All Time High" over the opening credits.

OCTOPUSSY		
Prologue:	5/5	(full credit for the AcroStar)
Plot:	10/30	
Villains:	5/15	(for Kahn, for the chutzpah to tell his henchman to toss 007 off a flying plane)
Bond Girls:	15/15	
FX:	18/20	
Cars:	0/10	
Music:	6/5	(for not using a song entitled "Octopussy")
# of Major Locations:	7	
Total: 66 of 100 points		

On Her Majesty's Secret Service

I almost took points away for the prologue of On Her Majesty's Secret Service. It's not so much as it's dull, but that it breaks a rule of good fiction. At the end of the prologue, after George Lazenby dispatches the bad guys, he turns to the camera and says, "That never happened to the other fellow," a reference to Sean Connery. *Why would James Bond say "that never happened to James Bond"?*

Seeing one James Bond plot, with few exceptions, is seeing them all. A megalomaniac plans to cause great havoc in the world to control what remains of his own Eden. However, what can intrigue us and thus make one plot better than another is the way the villain intends to gain control. In On Her Majesty's Secret Service, Ernst Stavro Blofeld plans to send beautiful, *brainwashed* women from his spa back to their hometowns to release biological pathogens into the world. The man is totally certifiable!

Diana Rigg has a strong showing in this film. Unlike many of the "Oh, James, sigh" girls, Tracy is strong and determined. Her transformation from a suicidal woman to a loving wife, underscored by Louis Armstrong's singing "We Have All the Time in the World," is a high point.

ON HER MAJESTY'S SECRET SERVICE		
Prologue:	0/5	(because of the inane remark)
Plot:	22/30	
Villains:	15/15	
Bond Girls:	20/15	(the classic Diana Rigg!)
FX:	0/20	(explosions and gunfire are it)
Cars:	0/10	(cable cars don't get points except in San Francisco)
Music:	7/5	(enough said)
# of Major Locations:	4	
Total: 68 of 100 points		

Live and Let Die

A winner in *Live and Let Die* is the cruel Mr. Big, leader of a drug smuggling ring. His henchman with the hook hand, Tee Hee, was one of those secondary characters who make villainy a remarkable contribution to the story. The film also boasts two excellent Bond girls, the supernatural Solitaire and double agent Rosie, the first black girl to become Bond's lover. Once again, Q supplies 007 with a particularly fortuitous buzz-saw watch used to save Bond, played for the first time in this film by Roger Moore, and Solitaire from death. And as I disagree with 007 about listening to the Beatles without earmuffs, the title song (technically not a Beatles song) sung by Paul McCartney and Wings is a strong contribution to the title sequence. (I usually wear earmuffs when listening to the music from the later films.)

LIVE AND LET DIE		
Prologue:	4/5	(interesting venues, but a bit over-the-top)
Plot:	15/30	
Villains:	15/15	
Bond Girls:	17/15	(bonus for Jane Seymour)
FX:	10/20	
Cars:	0/10	
Music:	6/5	
# of Major Locations:	4	
Total: 71 of 100 Points		

Tomorrow Never Dies

One of the highlights of *Tomorrow Never Dies* is Bond's BMW 750, a wheeled fortress with rockets, chain cutter, bulletproof glass, spike dispenser, and remote-controlled device in a cell phone. Just what every boy needs. Also a highlight is Teri Hatcher playing the elegant and sophisticated Paris Carver, wife of the evil Elliot Carver. I thought Carver's dream of dominating the news was about as bland as one could get, but he had his moments...like having his wife killed merely because she had been Bond's lover. Michelle Yeoh's tough Chinese spy, Wai Lin, proved a superb challenge for 007 to work with, which was a pleasure to watch.

TOMORROW NEVER DIES		
Prologue:	5/5	(knock-knock)
Plot:	5/30	
Villains:	10/15	
Bond Girls:	13/15	(both Wai Lin and Paris were different and interesting)
FX:	20/20	(the motorcycle run, the impossible helicopter hover)
Cars:	10/10	(that BMW)
Music:	4/5	
# of Major Locations:	8	
Total: 75 of 100 points		

Thunderball

The opening to *Thunderball* features Bond's escape from a castle by jet pack. For the first time, we see Ernst Stavro Blofeld as the villain Bond will face again in other films. SPECTRE steals nuclear weapons from a NATO bomber and uses them to extort money from the United States and England. Q provides a mini-aqualung and a Geiger counter watch (to locate the hidden bombs) and a jet pack, and the undersea action supplies dramatic special effects. Plus the title song was belted out, *really* belted out, by Tom Jones over the opening credits.

THUNDERBALL		
Prologue:	6/5	(bonus for the jet pack)
Plot:	20/30	
Villains:	15/15	
Bond Girls:	0/15	
FX:	20/20	(the underwater sequences)
Cars:	5/10	(the DB5's cameo appearance)
Music:	5/5	
# of Major Locations:	5	
Total: 76 of 100 points		

The World Is Not Enough

The World Is Not Enough continued EON's BMW mania, giving Bond an automobile that would suit a rock star. The plot revolves around stunning Elektra King, the daughter of an oil heiress and a recently slain British aristocrat. As Bond mentions, quoting the O'Neill play title, "*Mourning Becomes Electra*." She plans to use her secret lover, the criminal Renard, to explode an atomic weapon in a key shipping area, forcing the world to depend on her pipeline for oil. Much of the film displays what has become standard action for a 007 film with nothing unusual except for the final conflict between Bond and Renard where Bond handles radioactive rods with his bare hands to stop the atomic explosion.

THE WORLD IS NOT ENOUGH		
Prologue:	5/5	(the impossible chase, including the Thames boat and the hot air balloon)
Plot:	15/30	
Villains:	5/15	
Bond Girls:	14/15	
FX:	20/20	(hard to deny the spectacle)
Cars:	10/10	
Music:	4/5	
# of Major Locations:	7	
Total: 80 of 100 points		

Die Another Day

Enthusiasts who like action enjoy the opening to *Die Another Day*, with the hovercraft chase and 007 blowing up everything in sight. Although most Bond title sequences have a certain sameness about them, typically featuring silhouettes of shapely women, the sequence for *Die Another Day* is highly creative, with the figures alternating from fiery to icy.

Although she turns out to be a villain, Bond would have to search diligently for a more beautiful Bond girl than Rosamund Pike's Miranda Frost. And the Aston Martin V12 Vanquish appeared as an invisible car—quite a trick! (Pun intended.)

Die Another Day was an anthology of references to earlier Bond films: Q's laboratory testing early devices, John Cleese as Q ("I never joke about my work"), Halle Berry coming out of the sea like Ursula Andress, and the picture on the wall of the subway depicting the British sailor from the Player cigarette pack. The original came from Domino's four-page dialogue in Fleming's novel *Thunderball*. ("The man of my dreams," she says. "The sailor on the packet of Players.")

DIE ANOTHER DAY		
Prologue:	6/5	(although intended solely as an action piece, there's no denying it worked)
Plot:	10/30	
Villains:	10/15	
Bond Girls:	14/15	
FX:	20/20	(the ice palace, the glacier collapse and water ski, the car…)
Cars:	10/10	
Music:	3/5	(wear earmuffs)
# of Major Locations:	8	
Total: 81 of 100 points		

Diamonds Are Forever

In *Diamonds Are Forever*, SPECTRE is smuggling diamonds for use in a laser capable of firing from orbit, with which they plan to control the world. (Blofeld again. As I said before, the man is certifiable!) The Bond girls, unfortunately, don't measure up; Jill St. John as Tiffany Case starts out as a cool cookie but quickly deteriorates to the usual "Oh, James!" Plenty O'Toole at least provides a great line when she is tossed out the window of a high-rise hotel by a thug. (Bond mentions that it was a good shot because she landed in the swimming pool; the thug replies, "I didn't know there was a pool there.")

007 employed a piton gun in this movie, later used with great effect in *GoldenEye's* prologue. But the special effect that made the film was the car chase within the confines of a small parking lot, with an escape through a narrow alley. Bond's Ford Mustang drove through it tilted on two wheels. (The only problem? The Mustang entered the alley on one set of wheels and emerged on the opposite set.)

DIAMONDS ARE FOREVER		
Prologue:	5/5	
Plot:	20/30	
Villains:	10/15	(the sausage king didn't quite come across as threatening)
Bond Girls:	7/15	(awarded for Tiffany Case early in the film, and Bambi and Thumper later)
FX:	18/20	(although it's comical, I can't give full points because of the dubbed "shift" that switched the tilt of the Mustang)
Cars:	5/10	
Music:	5/5	
# of Major Locations:	12	(hyperactive with locations!)
Total: 82 of 100 points		

From Russia With Love

From Russia With Love is a favorite with many Bond admirers. In the very creepy prologue we are led to believe that 007 has been killed, strangled to death by Red Grant. Wristwatches have often played a big part in helping Bond in many of his adventures, but this time, in this murderous training exercise it is Grant who uses his watch for something other than telling time—he pulls a thin wire out of it and garrotes the man posing as Bond. Watch logic, by the way, is not always evident in the Bond films. In *Live and Let Die*, one watch is designed by MI6 to deflect bullets but in the demonstration with Bond, it *attracts* metal. That seems counterproductive!

If anything stands out in the Bond movies, it's the marvelous, zany, evil villains. They are all so creative, so sure of themselves, so self-righteous in their chosen paths of destructive criminal activity—and the utter efficiency of Red Grant as a professional killer makes him a worthy foe. But logic is not Grant's strong suit either. Pointing a gun at 007, Grant tells Bond he will be presumed a victim of suicide, then adds, "The first bullet won't kill you; neither will the second." What a way to commit suicide! Q provided 007 with a special briefcase (knife, tear gas, gold, folding rifle). And, instead of using *From Russia With Love* as the title song, the directors chose to have Matt Monro sing it within the story through Bond's car radio.

FROM RUSSIA WITH LOVE		
Prologue:	5/5	
Plot:	25/30	(the convolutions of SMERSH using Bond, Tatiana, MI6, and the KBG)
Villains:	15/15	(these were solid villains)
Bond Girls:	16/15	(extra point for model Daniela Bianchi as Tatiana)
FX:	15/20	
Cars:	1/10	(special point for the Orient Express wagon-lit cars as location)
Music:	6/5	(creative, using it internally)
# of Major Locations:	2	
Total: 85 of 100 points		

The Spy Who Loved Me

For sheer spectacle, the ski jump off the cliff in *The Spy Who Loved Me* with the Union Jack parachute has to be one of the best prologue stunts. (How *does* Q anticipate these needs?) Here, Stromberg attempts to precipitate a war between the United States and Russia by stealing both countries' nuclear submarines. The girl, Anya Amasova, Bond's counterpart in the KGB, has to work with him to prevent SPECTRE from succeeding.

The car, a fantastic Lotus Esprit that converts to a submarine, could lay mines and fire sea-to-air missiles! There is one beautiful villainess whom many felt should have had a larger role, the helicopter pilot, Naomi, but alas, 007 kills her after her brief appearance. In a musical departure from other films, *The Spy Who Loved Me*'s opening included Carly Simon singing a non-title song, "Nobody Does it Better."

THE SPY WHO LOVED ME		
Prologue:	6/5	(the woman's hands catching the Union Jack parachutist at the end of the prologue earns the extra point)
Plot:	20/30	(clever linkage, with MI6 and KGB "working together")
Villains:	10/15	
Bond Girls:	15/15	
FX:	17/20	(the Lotus submarine)
Cars:	10/10	(the Lotus non-submarine)
Music:	6/5	(Marvin Hamlisch)
# of Major Locations:	2	
Total: 86 0f 100 points		

For Your Eyes Only

While the *For Your Eyes Only* title sequence features the face of the singer, Sheena Easton, the prologue is otherwise less dramatic than most. On the other hand, the plot is a bit more complex and clever. Bond's "ally" is actually the bad guy who intends to steal the ATAC, a device that controls submarine Polaris missiles, while the initial villain, a Greek smuggler named Columbo, becomes Bond's ally. Super-car Lotus Esprit makes another appearance, but Bond uses a Citroen 2 CV *"deux cheveau"* for a car chase down a mountainside. Another exquisite Bond girl, Melina Havelock, is present to avenge the death of her father, a noted marine scientist who worked with MI6.

FOR YOUR EYES ONLY		
Prologue:	3/5	
Plot:	25/30	(complex plot, but centered on rather normal criminal situations)
Villains:	7/15	
Bond Girls:	15/15	(Melina! those eyes!)
FX:	13/20	
Cars:	10/10	
Music:	6/5	(the combination of Easton's voice and face in the title sequence)
# of Major Locations:	8	
Total: 87 of 100 points		

You Only Live Twice

Unlike many films where music unobtrusively soothes us during love scenes and hypes our blood pressure during action scenes, music often stands out in Bond films. From the Monty Norman twangy-guitar Bond theme that was introduced in *Dr. No*, to the signature title themes by mainstream artists, to the beautifully crafted John Barry scores, James Bond music is always recognizable. One of the most haunting and beautiful of these was Barry's *You Only Live Twice*, sung by Nancy Sinatra during the title sequence.

In *You Only Live Twice*, Asian women were featured for the first time with beautiful Japanese actresses Akiko Wakabayashi and Mie Hama playing opposite 007. Bond is made up to look Japanese and assumes the role of the husband to "Kissy," who in reality is a Japanese secret agent there to help Bond find the hidden SPECTRE rocket base. Q supplies Little Nellie, a gyro-copter with built-in offensive and defensive weapons used by Bond in a successful aerial battle with SPECTRE helicopters. Incidentally, the screenwriter on this film was Roald Dahl! Yes, *that* Roald Dahl.

YOU ONLY LIVE TWICE		
Prologue:	5/5	
Plot:	20/30	(Bond going undercover as Japanese)
Villains:	15/15	(devious, technical, determined)
Bond Girls:	15/15	(the actresses worked hard on the English script—and were total babes)
FX:	20/20	(Little Nellie, the rocket base—hokey but fun villainy)
Cars:	0/10	
Music:	6/5	(beautiful title melody)
# of Major Locations:	9	
Total: 90 of 100 points		

Licence to Kill

Licence to Kill was Dalton's second and final outing as Bond. I liked this picture. I liked the cleverness of Sanchez, the main villain, with his escape plan and money-raising scam. His young henchman, Dario, also stood out as a ruthless and chilling sidekick. Carey Lowell was refreshing, competent and a total babe as the Bond girl. The comic relief by Wayne Newton was wonderfully underplayed. The gadgets and equipment were low-key as well (a manta-ray cloak, a cummerbund with concealed rope, and a Piper Cub–sized airplane!) and employed to great effect. The only nod to the spectacular was the massive semi-trailer tilting up on two wheels as the rocket whizzed beneath it.

LICENCE TO KILL		
Prologue:	5/5	(good action and a fun ending parachuting into the wedding)
Plot:	20/30	
Villains:	15/15	(their goal, running a drug ring, was a more reasonable villainy than the usual megalomania)
Bond Girls:	20/15	(bonus for the refreshing Bond girl)
FX:	20/20	(because most was believable; I overlook the truck thing as spectacle)
Cars:	5/10	
Music:	4/5	
# of Major Locations:	6	
Total: 95 of 100 points		

GoldenEye

With a 640-foot bungee-cord jump down the face of a dam, followed by a battle with a Russian garrison, followed by a motorcycle chase of an airplane over a cliff, the introduction of Pierce Brosnan as James Bond in *GoldenEye* is intense; returning Shirley Bassey for the title song was a nice touch of *Goldfinger* nostalgia. Maybe I was just hungry to see Bond in action again, but I enjoyed this film. The Aston Martin DB5 is back for a cameo appearance. Then there is the eye-popping red Ferrari 355 driven by the equally eye-popping Xenia Onatopp (played by Dutch actress Famke Janssen).

Alec Trevelyan, formerly MI6's agent 006, was suitably treacherous as a turncoat. The well-staged fight scene with 007 forces the viewer to use some imagination since it was shot in partial darkness. I didn't find Trevelyan's motive for turning against Britain convincing, but he is convincingly evil. His ICBM train is ugly and brutal-looking, a perfect piece of equipment. The Russian girl, Natalia, is pretty and vulnerable without being too "Oh, James!" Q provides enough equipment to make it all interesting, providing Bond with a pen grenade and a piton gun (its second appearance). All in all, if you could get over Brosnan, not Connery or Moore, being Bond, it was a highly competent film.

GOLDENEYE		
Prologue:	6/5	(that opening jump!)
Plot:	19/30	
Villains:	14/15	(Famke)
Bond Girls:	20/15	(Famke)
FX:	20/20	(a lot of spectacle, even if some of it was unbelievable)
Cars:	12/10	(the DB5 and the Ferarri)
Music:	4/5	
# of Major Locations:	5	
Total: 100 of 100 points		

Goldfinger

I clearly remember one 1964 evening in Chelmsford, Massachusetts, standing in a long line of people outside the cinema waiting for the doors to open for a new movie called *Goldfinger*. Although I had not seen the previous films, I had read all the Ian Fleming books and was as hyped as the publicity about the film. Sitting in the darkened theater, I was mesmerized as the white dots marched across the screen to the four stinging darts of music followed by the twanging of the 007 theme. The gun barrel led to the wavering dot that opened on the duck swimming toward the dock...I had entered the magic world of 007.

Goldfinger started strong and never let up. The prologue alone propels the viewer into *everything* that is James Bond. There is danger, sophistication, gadgetry, sex, spectacle, action, and gallows humor ("Shocking, positively shocking"). And the film that follows builds on every one of those elements. For the first time in a Bond film, all those diamonds that are the symbols of the Bond franchise came together in spades. The title sequence uses the girl's gold-covered body as a projection screen on which to depict scenes from this and previous films. Shirley Bassey's *brassy* treatment of the title song sets the hard-edged tone of Goldfinger's character, and the title music is often repeated during subsequent scenes, sometimes mixed with the 007 theme, in a highly effective use of orchestration. The opening of the story in Miami illustrates Bond's decisive character; he not only understands Goldfinger's cheating nature and uses it against him, but also uses his considerable charm to win over Goldfinger's Girl Friday, Jill Masterson.

To learn how Goldfinger is smuggling gold, 007 pursues Goldfinger's elegant 1937 Rolls Royce from England to the continent. The trip is not only clever for its tracking gadget, but it is also beautifully photographed in the Swiss mountains. During the chase scene in Goldfinger's gold-processing plant, as in Pussy Galore's aerial spraying scene toward the end of the film, John Barry's score sets an action-in-progress theme that contributes to the excitement. By contrast, the morbid theme he composed to introduce Oddjob's appearances is especially tragic when he launches his deadly hat to kill Tilly Masterson.

Oddjob, played by Hawaiian wrestler Harold Sakata, was an extraordinary villain! Always silent, bizarre in appearance in a tight formal suit, he wears a bowler hat that can slice through a statue's neck. Oddjob is invincible with his enormous strength that can crush a golf ball and take blows from a heavy bar of gold bullion. Goldfinger himself seems unstoppable in his quest to control the world's gold market by invading Fort Knox and exploding a radioactive device. The plot is unique in the way Goldfinger intends to dominate the world economically. Goldfinger also has the honor of uttering one of the most famous lines of any Bond film just before he is about to turn 007 into a contralto, "No, Mr. Bond, I expect you to die."

When Bond is on Goldfinger's jet there is a passing reference to Q's gadget-filled briefcase from the previous film, but the first of this film's spectacular Bond gadgets is the Aston Martin DB5 with its bulletproof glass, oil ejecting spray, smokescreen ability, revolving license plates ("valid in all countries"), tire-slashing hubcaps, front-firing machine guns, and—everyone's favorite—the passenger ejection seat.

The main Bond girl is, of course, Pussy Galore. Honor Blackman, best known at the time for her role in the British program *The Avengers*, is introduced rather late in the film but clearly makes her mark with her name, her appearance and the fact that she is "immune" to Bond's charms. However, he does break through her icy exterior and converts her to heterosexuality with a single encounter in a horse barn. (Nobody does it better!)

GOLDFINGER		
Prologue:	10/5	(for everything!)
Plot:	40/30	(unique)
Villains:	25/15	(villains galore!)
Bond Girls:	25/15	(five bonus points for Tilly Masterson alone)
FX:	25/20	(crushing the Lincoln Continental definitely worth the extra points)
Cars:	25/10	(DB5)
Music:	10/5	(brassy Bassey)
# of Major Locations:	7	
Total: 167 of 100 points		

Goldfinger is not, of course, without its flaws. An obvious problem is the way Pussy Galore's Flying Circus "gassed" Fort Knox. Getting the entire population in on the ruse in such a short time without the media or Goldfinger finding out is unrealistic. Also, it takes the gas a few seconds to kill the thugs when released in a sealed chamber, while merely spraying gas over the fort instantly drops marching troops. (Are nonmilitary aircraft even allowed to fly over Fort Knox at that height?) There was also a major error in photographic framing when Bond uses the tire-chomping hubcap to disable Tilly Masterson's Mustang. Bond comments on it being a bad coincidence that two tires blew out. They both ignore the obviously slashed metal all along the side of the car, clearly visible to the audience. It may be picky to mention, but when Bond mentions their close call ("Three more seconds and...."), the clock on the Fort Knox bomb had obviously stopped at 007 seconds. He can determine the half-life of radioactive material in his mind but can't count up to 007?

Goldfinger is the obvious winner when it comes to what it takes to make a Bond film a *Bond Film*! How can one argue with quantified logic?

Bias! What bias?

———

RAY DEMPSEY lives in Palo Alto, California. During his career he taught high-school and college-level classes, worked in sales and marketing in publishing and the airlines industry, and most recently served as customs compliance manager in high tech before retiring. He holds degrees from Emerson College, Boston; marketing (summa cum laude) from Clark University; and an MBA from Babson College. He has published in Monogram Aviation Publications and contributed articles to the Ian Fleming Web site. Ray has traveled extensively in the United States, Asia, and Europe where, in Holland, he had the good fortune to meet his beautiful wife, Anneke, his partner for over thirty-four years.

What Are the Best and Worst Gadgets from Q Branch?

DON'T PRESS THAT BUTTON!
A Practical Potential Buyer's Guide to Bond's Gadgets

IF YOUR FIRST EXPOSURE to James Bond happened before the age of nine, you probably fell in love with the series for one reason: the gadgets.

The women were hot, but you wouldn't care about that for a few more years. James Bond was tough and could fight, but so could those short guys on UHF's Samurai Saturday, and they had the added appeal of speaking without their lips matching up to their words. Global politics, espionage, and undercover infiltrations *still* aren't interesting, years later.

No, the thing that made your prepubescent brain scream with unrestrained joy was all the cool stuff Bond picked up in Q Branch. You wanted the grappling-hook pistol, and the pen filled with acid, and the laser watch, and the hand-held suction cups for climbing walls, and the wrist dart gun, and the rappelling cummerbund—even though you had no idea what a cummerbund was.

But now that you're all grown up, do the gadgets still have the same appeal? Do you still wish you could run to the nearest Wal-Mart and buy an electric razor that can deliver a close shave plus sweep your room for electronic listening devices?

This practical guide will look at some of the best of Bond's gadgets, and offer valuable buying advice to those interested in plunking down their hard-earned dollars for spy gear.

GADGET: False-bottom briefcase which holds a magnetic mine, used by Bond in *Octopussy*.

USES: Protecting and transporting papers, blowing things up.

COOLNESS: Hidden compartments are always cool. So are mines.

REALITY: These already exist, in a wide variety of colors and payloads.

DO YOU WANT IT?: Yes, you do. Think about how memorable your next corporate meeting will be if you're carrying one of these.

SAFETY TIP: Don't try to bring it through airport security.

GADGET: Snorkel that looks like a seagull, used by Bond in *Goldfinger*.

USES: Fool your friends at the pool, see other seagulls up close, collect change from the bottom of public fountains.

COOLNESS: Uncool. The crocodile submarine in *Octopussy* has many more applications. In fact, so does simple scuba gear. Q Branch was apparently hitting the NyQuil when they thought this one up.

REALITY: Possible to manufacture, but tough to market, depending on where you put your lips.

DO YOU WANT IT?: Not really, except to amuse yourself while drinking too much.

HYGIENE TIP: Boil the bird after every use.

GADGET: Ski pole that fires a rocket, used in *The Spy Who Loved Me*.

USES: Improve your slalom time, blow up your friends, roast a chicken really fast.

COOLNESS: Very cool.

REALITY: Single use wouldn't be practical; it would be too heavy, and it might go off too soon (many men have this problem, and it's nothing to be embarrassed about).

DO YOU WANT IT?: Yes, but you should be careful—tucking high explosives under your arm while speeding 70 mph downhill isn't for anyone under the age of fourteen.

SAFETY TIP: Practice on the bunny slope before you take it down that black diamond run.

GADGET: Aston Martin DB5 sports car, used by Bond in *Goldfinger*, *Thunderball*, *GoldenEye*, and *Tomorrow Never Dies*.

USES: The ultimate road rage machine/babe magnet: oil-slick sprayer, smoke screens, tire-slashing blades, machine guns, and an ejector seat for when your blind date turns out to be a bore.

COOLNESS: This is one pimped-out ride.

REALITY: You could probably pay to have this car custom made, but it would cost a lot of money, and you wouldn't be allowed to drive it anywhere, except maybe in Texas.

DO YOU WANT IT?: Hell, yeah. Rush hour would never be the same.

BUYING TIP: At the dealer, don't be afraid to haggle. And don't get suckered into buying the undercarriage rust protection.

GADGET: Stick-on third nipple, used by Bond in *The Man with the Golden Gun*.

USES: For those many times in life when you just need a third nipple.

COOLNESS: At first glance, not very cool. But once you consider the possibilities (see below), the coolness factor rises, much more so than the fake fingerprints Bond used in *Diamonds Are Forever*.

REALITY: Hollywood SPFX guys make these all the time, and you can too with some plaster for an impression cast, and some foam latex. *Hint*: Shave your chest first.

DO YOU WANT IT?: Yes. Put them on sofas, on jewelry, on windows, on fruit, and all over yourself before that visit to the public pool.

SAFETY TIP: Don't use Super glue.

GADGET: Little Nellie portable gyrocopter with rocket launchers, machine guns, flamethrower, and heat-seeking missiles from *You Only Live Twice*.

USES: Fly around, impress the ladies, drop stuff on people.

COOLNESS: Übercool. Smaller than a helicopter. Not nearly as expensive to use as the Bell-Trexton rocket pack Bond used in *Thunderball*, and with a lot more firepower.

REALITY: Available on eBay for under 20k, but without the weaponry. (Weaponry is available separately on eBay.)

DO YOU WANT IT?: Of course you want it. Just think about all the stuff you could drop on people.

SAFETY TIP: From three hundred feet, a small honeydew melon can cripple a man.

GADGET: Wristwatch with plastic explosive and detonator, used by Bond in *Moonraker*.

USES: Blow stuff up, threaten to blow stuff up.

COOLNESS: Cool. Blowing stuff up never gets old.

REALITY: Possible, and cheap to make. But you'd have to buy refills all the time. They always get you on the refills.

DO YOU WANT IT?: Yes. *Excuse me, what time is it? It's time to blow stuff up!* Let's start with that stupid seagull snorkel.

SAFETY TIP: Don't play with all the dials until you've read the instructions.

GADGET: Keys that open ninety percent of the world's locks, used by Bond in *The Living Daylights*.

USES: Unlimited: Steal cars. Rob banks. Take the change from parking meters. Shop after hours. And never pay for a vending machine again.

COOLNESS: Opening stuff up: cool. Walking around like a janitor with a big key ring: uncool.

REALITY: Master keys exist, and can be found on the Internet. So can lock picks. So can lawyers, which you'll need after you get caught opening up other people's locks.

DO YOU WANT IT?: No. You'd probably just lose them.

SAFETY TIP: Don't keep these in your back pocket while ice skating. Or your front pocket.

GADGET: Surfboard with concealed explosives, combat knife, and mini-computer, used by Bond in *Die Another Day*.

USES: Hang ten, then kill seven.

COOLNESS: Super cool. You can shred that gnarly barrel, and at the same time Google what the hell that means.

REALITY: It's possible to produce, but be careful you don't wax your mini-computer.

DO YOU WANT IT?: Of course. But instead of weapons and electronics, you can fill your board with soda and snacks (that you got for free at the vending machine).

SAFETY TIP: Make sure the combat knife is properly secured before you hit the waves, or you'll be hanging nine.

GADGET: X-Ray glasses, used by Bond in *The World Is Not Enough.*

USES: Seeing though things like playing cards, safes, walls, doors, and clothing (to look for concealed weapons and stick-on third nipples).

COOLNESS: Perhaps Bond's coolest gadget. It would sure make everyday life a lot more interesting.

REALITY: If you ever sent away for a pair of these in the back of a comic book, you know they don't work, but what did you expect for $2.95? Your mother told you they wouldn't work, didn't she? Real versions may exist, but they probably cost big bucks. And cause cancer.

DO YOU WANT IT?: Sure you do. Just don't take them to family reunions. Or retirement homes.

COMFORT TIP: Wear baggy pants.

GADGET: Underwater manta ray cloak, used by Bond in *Licence to Kill.*

USES: Pretend you're a manta ray, get close to other manta rays, get sexually assaulted by a manta ray.

COOLNESS: Not cool, unless you have a secret thing for manta rays.

REALITY: Can be made in real life, but for God's sake, why?

DO YOU WANT IT?: Only if you're really lonely. You might also consider getting the seagull snorkel as well, and pretend you're a ray chasing a seagull. You can play that one for hours and hours.

BUYING TIP: If you spend more that $30 for this, you're a real moron.

GADGET: Lotus Esprit sports car that turns into a submarine, complete with mines, missiles, underwater ink jets, and self-destruct mechanism, that Bond used in *The Spy Who Loved Me* and *For Your Eyes Only*.

USES: Never take the ferry again, drive into swimming pool to fetch the quarters Grandpa throws in there.

COOLNESS: A hot car, and a hot submersible, all in one. Plus rockets.

REALITY: Boat cars do exist in real life, but they're actually dorky looking, and driven by people who can't get dates.

DO YOU WANT IT?: You know you do. But when purchasing options, go for an Alpine stereo and Bose speakers instead of a self-destruct button—it's more practical.

UNDERWATER TIP: If you drive over a starfish and cut it in half, it will grow into two new starfishes, both of them very pissed off at you.

GADGET: Dinner jacket which turns into a black sniper's outfit, used by Bond in *The Living Daylights* and *Licence to Kill*.

USES: When black tie events become boring.

COOLNESS: Cooler than the light blue tux with the ruffle shirt which turns into an adult diaper, but not by much.

REALITY: They already have these for rent at Gingiss. You'll need two forms of ID, and there's a mandatory fourteen-day waiting period.

DO YOU WANT IT?: You don't want to admit it, but yes, you do. But then, you never had much taste in clothing.

FASHION TIP: Belts are okay, but the trendy sniper prefers suspenders.

GADGET: Cigarette lighter grenade, used by Bond in *Tomorrow Never Dies*.

USES: No smoking *means* no smoking.

COOLNESS: Anything that blows up is cool (see *plastic explosive watch*).

REALITY: You can put explosives into anything: lighters, bottles, cans, small animals, etc.

DO YOU WANT IT?: Absolutely. Think about taking it to a heavy metal concert for when the power ballad is playing.

SAFETY TIP: Don't get it confused with your real lighter, because you might accidentally throw your real lighter at the bad guys and they'll say, "Why'd you throw a lighter at us, stupid? Are we supposed to be scared?" Also, you might blow your face off.

GADGET: Piton gun with retractable wire, used by Bond in *Diamonds Are Forever* and *GoldenEye*.

USES: Climb up buildings and rock faces, retrieve the remote control without getting up from the couch.

COOLNESS: Climbing, swinging, and shooting things are all cool.

REALITY: Wouldn't actually be strong enough to hold a man's weight, but you could have fun letting your buddies try it out.

DO YOU WANT IT?: Yes. It's like being Spider-Man, but without the web-by discharge.

SAFETY TIP: Don't point it at your own face, or at family members, unless you're trying to climb them.

GADGET: Exploding talcum powder tear gas, used by Bond in *From Russia With Love*.

USES: Personal hygiene, making enemies cry.

COOLNESS: Talc isn't very cool. Neither is tear gas. But it does explode, which counts for something.

REALITY: It might already exist. It might not. Who cares?

DO YOU WANT IT?: No. You make your significant other cry all the time without gas, and no one uses talc anymore.

SAFETY TIP: Wear a gas mask before applying to your underarms.

GADGET: Magnetic watch with circular saw, used by Bond in *Live and Let Die*.

USES: Cutting through rope tied around your wrists, finding screws you dropped on the carpeting.

COOLNESS: Having your watch face spin around really fast is cool. Cutting off your own hand at the wrist is uncool.

REALITY: Buy a chainsaw that tells time instead. It's cheaper and more effective.

DO YOU WANT IT?: No. If you want a cool Bond timepiece, get the plastic explosive watch. Or the laser beam watch from *Tomorrow Never Dies*. Or the grappling-hook watch from *The World Is Not Enough*. Or the ticker tape message watch from *The Spy Who Loved Me*. Or the digital radio watch from *For Your Eyes Only*. Or even the Geiger counter watch from *Thunderball*—you can't have too many Geiger counters around the house.

SAFETY TIP: Careful you don't lose any fingers when you reset for different time zones.

Remember: You're never too old to play with toys. Especially explosive, potentially deadly, extremely expensive toys. Just think about how envious your friends and family will be when they see you driving around in your sporty new BMW 750 iL with the electrified door handles, bulletproof glass, reinflating tires, and rear nail ejectors.

Go ahead. Think about it. Because that's as close as you'll ever get to owning one, spy-boy.

Now go boil your seagull snorkel—that thing is riddled with germs.

JA KONRATH is the author of a wildly successful thriller series about Chicago cop Lt. Jack Daniels, which includes *Whiskey Sour, Bloody Mary, Rusty Nail*, and the forthcoming *Dirty Martini*. Joe's stories and essays have appeared in many magazines and anthologies. He lives in the suburbs, has one wife, three kids (that he knows of), and a few dogs. Visit him at www.JAKonrath.com.

ERIN DAILEY AND HARRY ELLIOTT

Who Is the Sexiest Bond Girl?

"My Name Is Coochie McPantsless, What's Yours?"
Our Top Ten Bond Girls of All Time

WHAT MAKES A BOND movie a Bond movie? Is it the opening sequence with Bond in the bloody iris and the all-too-familiar accompanying theme music? Is it a consistently amusing and bemused Q with his array of spy gadgets and gear? Is it the Aston Martins and BMW coupes and Versace tuxes and diamond cufflinks and martinis shaken-not-stirred? Is it the super-villains with the whacked-out hair and/or teeth who are set on world domination?

The simple answer is: all of the above.

These things are all essential to the "Bondishness" of a Bond movie. But let's face it, even with all of these elements intact, a Bond movie would not be a Bond movie without one teeny-tiny, itty-bitty little thing.

The Bond girls.

A Bond movie without at least two Bond girls is simply not a Bond movie. The Bond girl is a special breed of beast that is specific only to the Bond Movie. They simply don't exist anywhere *but* the Bond universe. Really, where else could you come across a never-ending supply of women who are gorgeous, dangerous, possibly duplicitous, occasionally helpless, often expendable, and who have really nice racks?

What? We're not being rude. Bond girls are hot. They're supposed to be hot. And they're supposed to have nice racks. We can say that. There is no political correctness in the Bond universe, thank you very much. So don't get all up in our kitchens and demand that we refer to the Bond girls as Bond Women. They're not women. They're girls. Chicks. Babes. Hussies. Hell, ninety percent of the Bond girls drop trou before you can even say "007," and that's hardly the behavior of a woman. That's the behavior of a girl who is a figment of the overactive imagination of men worldwide. And we're totally okay with that.

The Bond girls rock, and we all have our favorites. Even if you aren't a huge fan of the Bond movies, you still have a favorite Bond girl. You could be an old-school fan, like Harry, who happens to be a lover of all things kitsch, and who finds himself gravitating toward the Bond girls with the 'fros and caftans, or you could be more of a new-school fan, like Erin, who gained a charter membership in the Good Ol' Boys Club when she exclaimed, "I totally don't buy Denise Richards as a nuclear expert—*Whoa. Nice rack*, Richards!"

Our favorites may not match up with yours, but who gives a damn? There are plenty of Bond girls to go around.

Ursula Andress as "Honey Ryder" in *Dr. No*

HARRY: Oh, honey, please.

ERIN: Shut up.

HARRY: Honey Ryder? That's where you start? Honey "I Was Born of the Surf for I Am a Goddess" Ryder?

ERIN: You need to shut up immediately. Before you get all, "Oh, of *course* you have Honey on your list! She's the first Bond girl!" I'll have you know that she is *not* officially the first Bond girl. She's actually the second. The first one is Sylvia Trench, and if that isn't the worst name ever for a Bond girl then I don't know what is. Fortunately for Honey, old Trenchmouth doesn't burst forth from the sea like a modern-day Venus on the damn half shell, so she's easily forgotten.

The beauty of Honey Ryder doesn't begin and end with her white hipster bikini and conveniently attached knife. No, her appeal runs much deeper than that. For one thing, she has an awesome backstory that involves a murdered marine biologist father and a rape by a landlord. Honey gets revenge on the landlord by sticking a black widow spider under his mosquito net, and it takes the guy a week to die. How bitchin' is that? So, she's beautiful, independent, and lethal? Works for me.

At the time Honey Ryder rose from the foam wearing nothing but a bikini and a smile, women didn't appear onscreen in bikinis. They just didn't. So with that one small move, ol' Honey made us understand that the Bond movies weren't going to be your run-of-the-mill celluloid experience. No sir. Cubby Broccoli came to play, thank you very much, and the name of the game was "Hot Chicks in Bikinis and the British Spies Who Dig Them."

Donna Garratt and Trina Parks as "Bambi" and "Thumper" in *Diamonds Are Forever*

HARRY: I have to say, not so impressed with your first choice.

ERIN: Who asked you?

HARRY: Well, obviously *someone* asked or we wouldn't be doing this in the first place.

ERIN: Good point. Well, if my first choice is so disappointing, what're *you* stepping up to the plate with, huh?

HARRY: A much bolder choice, my friend. White bikinis and hip knives? *Yawn.* I'm more fond of the bizarro, campy '70s-style Bond girls who started showing up around the time that Sean Connery began contemplating getting his paychecks from someone other than Cubby Broccoli.

Often, the girls in Bond films function simply as set dressing—like a jiggling nymph at the pool or the tarty assistant in Q's laboratory bringing by a cup of tea. Just slightly higher on the Bond girl hierarchy are "characters" like Bambi and Thumper. Their whole scene could be deleted from the film without notice, but what they lack in anything resembling character development they make up for in ass-kicking fun—with Bond's ass on the receiving end of those size six lace-up go-go boots.

The scene in which 007 meets up with this scantily clad duo takes place in a postmodern concrete and glass house that's doubling as a prison for the Howard Hughes–inspired tycoon, Willard Whyte (played by famed sausage monger, Jimmy Dean, which—the hell?). Bambi (in crazy braids, head wrap, and choker necklace) and Thumper (in yellow bikini, midriff chain, and hoop earrings) are, I think, his prison guards. What, is it "Casual Friday" at the All-White Prison of Pork Product Purveyors? Also, why is Bambi hiding behind a chair and Thumper lounging on a large rock? Are they there to clean the house? Perhaps Avon Ladies at the wrong address? Tupperware? Amway? It's never explained, so fill in the blank yourself.

At first, it appears Bond has lucked into his first onscreen ménage à trois, and an interracial one at that. But wait—it's 1971 and we can't handle that yet. Let's bring on the violence instead.

And rather than pulling a gun or a knife on Bond (yawn, boring), Bambi and Thumper bring on the...gymnastics! Front flips, cartwheels, and chandelier hanging abound. A glass coffee table meets its maker. All three end up in the pool. Why, you may ask? Because it looks *awesome*, that's why.

Jill St. John as "Tiffany Case" in *Diamonds Are Forever*

ERIN: I can't believe that you have a movie like *Diamonds* in front of you and you go with the *eye candy*.

HARRY: What? The Bond girls very often *are* eye candy. Or haven't you noticed?

ERIN: Oh, I've noticed. But at least *my* choice for my second favorite Bond girl isn't a lowly "prison guard" named after an animated woodland creature.

HARRY: Jill St. John? You're countering with Jill St. John? And this somehow makes you *better* than me?

ERIN: Dude. She makes her first appearance in champagne-colored underwear and a bouffant hairdo that defies the natural laws of gravity. And the hair keeps changing color and style throughout the entire movie! During her first scene alone she goes from a blonde to a brunette to a redhead! And she apparently owns stock in a wig company *and* Aqua Net, because *damn*. She's also savvy and world-wise and doesn't throw Bond into bed within seconds of meeting him, preferring not to mix business with pleasure. Of course, she doesn't know he's Bond when she first meets him, so this could be why she doesn't shag him right away. Bond girl panties tend to fall right off after hearing the first utterance of "Bond. James Bond."

Come on, Harry. The only other Bond girl in the movie is the hilariously named Plenty O'Toole. And, yeah, even though her self-introduction at the craps table ("Hi, I'm Plenty!" Bond's dry response? "Of course you are." Heh.) almost steals the film, she can't hold a candle to St. John's spicy, diamond-stealing redhead.

HARRY: Hee. I forgot about "Plenty O'Toole." What a disaster.

ERIN: Amen.

Barbara Bach as "Major Anya Amasova" in
The Spy Who Loved Me

HARRY: Major Amasova (a.k.a. "Agent XXX" before Vin Diesel ruined that moniker forever) is one of my favorite Bond girls because she is so unintentionally laughable. Poor thing. It's like the harder she tries to be a badass super Commie, the more she comes across like Mr. Magoo in a supermodel costume. For example, she knocks out Bond with a fake cigarette gadget and steals some microfilm from him, right? Wrong. In the next scene, Bond wakes up and heads to MI6 in Cairo, only to discover that M, XXX, and her boss, General Gogol, are together waiting for him. So... why did Barbie knock him out, exactly? So she could beat him to the office in the morning?

Her incompetence climaxes (hee!) toward the end of the movie, as Bond and the U.S. Navy are trying to bust out of Stromberg's giant submarine-eating tanker. Agent XXX has been taken prisoner and is tied to a white chaise lounge with about a foot of... is that bungee cord? I guess the titanium prison cell surrounded by three feet of razor wire was all booked up.

Agent XXX fully wins my heart at the conclusion of the film, when she finds out that Bond killed her previous lover and she vows revenge... which she totally doesn't follow through on, because faster than you can say, "Sergei who?" she's naked and doing Bond in the floating bubble glider. What a bimbo.

Famke Janssen as "Xenia Zaragevna Onatopp" in *GoldenEye*

ERIN: See, this is where I think we fundamentally diverge in what makes a Bond girl a favorite: You like them useless but amusing, and I like them ass-kicking with great wardrobes.

HARRY: Hm. You could be right on that.

ERIN: I mean, this is why I love Xenia Onatopp in *Golden*—

HARRY: Wait one minute. You can't pick Xenia Onatopp. She's a *villain*.

ERIN: I *don't care*. As far as I'm concerned, Famke Janssen is the hottest Bond girl of all time. She's Russian (okay, Georgian, whatever), she smokes cigars, she flies helicopters, she drives like a maniac, and she breaks men's backs *as a form of foreplay*. There's something intensely wrong with her and yet, every time she's onscreen, I find myself wondering what it would feel like if she stuck her tongue in my ear. And then floored me with an uppercut to the jaw, obviously, because the woman is fierce. The scene in which she and Bond fling each other around the sauna is one of the sexiest and most violent love scenes ever committed to celluloid. And I even love it when she flips the visor down over her kohl-lined eyes right before she hijacks that 'copter.

My favorite scene in the whole movie may very well be the moment when Xenia shoots the hell out of everyone at the GoldenEye satellite station or whatever the hell it is and gets visibly, um, *excited* while doing so. She *shoots* people and has *multiple orgasms*. And her companion, that Russian general with a shoe for a nose, just looks at her like, "Okay. No more shooting for you." She rules.

HARRY: Yeah. You're right. She rules. Now I'm just pissed that I didn't pick her.

ERIN: *Ha!*

Jane Seymour as "Solitaire" in *Live and Let Die*

HARRY: My fave Bond girls not only bring their good looks and curves to the spy vs. spy party, they also bring a little mystery. That's the sole reason that Jane Seymour's Solitaire makes an appearance in my top five Bond girls of all time list. Well, that and she's a tarot-card-reading virgin psychic who works for a heroin-manufacturing, voodoo-loving criminal mastermind named Dr. Kananga. Who comes up with this crap?

Solitaire starts out all businesslike, using her mad tarot card skillz to track the freshly minted Bond, Roger Moore, on a flight to New York for her boss, Dr. Kananga. But trouble starts brewing for her when she later reads Bond's tarot cards at the Fillet of Soul restaurant in Harlem.

ERIN: Hee. "Fillet of Soul." Seriously. I love these movies.

HARRY: I know, right? So she reads his cards and then Bond chooses the Lovers card out of the deck and is all, "Us?" with an arched eyebrow and Solitaire is all, "*I am a virgin psychic!*" and Bond is all, "*Look at my arched eyebrow!*" and right there, you just know she ain't gonna be a virgin for long. Hell, you can use a stopwatch to time that downfall.

Bond, of course, beds her, and the inevitable side effect is that she loses all psychic ability. It doesn't take Kananga long to figure out she's now about as psychic as a Magic 8-Ball, so Bond spends the rest of the damn movie trying to rescue her. But I don't really care, because I love Solitaire's fixation on heavy liquid eyeliner and crazy Cleopatraesque costumes, and these things make her my favorite of

ASK DR. YES

Dear Dr. Yes,

I'm desperate to seduce Mr. Bond. I've seen him many times but have never caught his attention. How do I get him to notice me? How did you do it?

Desperately Seeking James

P.S. I've enclosed a photograph so you can see that I am worthy.

Dear Desperate,

You are adequate, yes.

There are only two sure ways to get James's attention. One is to get a job working for an evil genius bent on world domination. He'll sleep with you, but then he'll probably kill you. The other is to get a job as a spy working for a rival power that then forms a tense but cooperative relationship with MI6 to achieve a common goal. He'll sleep with you, but will probably kill your current husband and/or lover. Not as bad, but still a downside.

If you don't have or can't get either of these positions, I have one suggestion for you: cleavage. He's a sucker for it.

As for how I landed James, it was love at first sight.

JAMES: Bond, James Bond. And you are?
ME: Wilsuk.
JAMES: Wilsuk? Indeed?
ME: Yes. (pause) Dr. Wilsuk. Yes.
JAMES: Well, perhaps a demonstration in my room. . . .

I had him at hello.

the "Damsel in Distress" Bond girls who would be roadkill without 007's gallant assistance.

Michelle Yeoh as "Wai Lin" in *Tomorrow Never Dies*

ERIN: God, I loves me some Michelle Yeoh.
HARRY: Michelle Yeoh? You picked Michelle Yeoh? What about the Hatcher?!

ERIN: Teri Hatcher? You thought I'd pick Teri Hatcher? Are you *high*?

HARRY: I... may be. But that is not the point!

ERIN: Oh, I think it *is* the point, my friend. Because Teri Hatcher, even while in possession of her old "they're spectacular" boobs fame instead of her current physique that reminds us of a Barbie crafted out of matchstick pretzels, does less than nothing for me in this movie. Nada. Zip. Zilch. Zero. Seriously—when you have to choose between a Bond girl who can kick Bond's ass three ways to Sunday and a Bond girl whose only talent is sucking the olive out of the bottom of a martini glass from three feet away, you go with the ass-kicking Bond girl every time. Or, at least, I do. And my opinion is the only one that matters, so shut up.

HARRY: I—

ERIN: Shut up. Also? Shut up. Michelle Yeoh kicks all kinds of arse in this movie and I love that she's slightly older than your average Bond girl. But, then, I'm a chick, and we tend to be all, "You go girl!" about women of a certain age who can do an airborne propeller kick while handcuffed to Pierce Brosnan and still look hot doing it. Also? Wai and James bicker through most of their scenes together instead of doing the usual double entendre–filled flirting crap that Bond and his chosen Bond girl usually engage in, and their snappy repartee is all sorts of entertaining. They're like a hyperviolent version of Gable and Lombard. With jujitsu.

Maud Adams as "Octopussy" in *Octopussy*

HARRY: Hee. Octopussy.

ERIN: Hee. Octopussy.

HARRY: Why? Why can't I type or say that name without giggling?

ERIN: Because you're twelve.

HARRY: True.

ERIN: That's okay. I'm twelve too.

HARRY: I mean, it's a terrible, horrible, awful, hilarious, perfect name. I think only someone as gorgeous as Maud Adams could have pulled this off. As the title character she's all fabulous blue eyes and pouty, sultry lips, and is constantly swathed in an amazing collection of pastel saris. Hott. Adams also gets bonus points in my book as being the only actress to have not one but two Bond girl roles under her low-slung belt. Her first Bond girl role was as the easily seduced and quickly murdered Andrea Anders in the 1974 film *The Man with the*

Golden Gun. The Anders role is an afterthought, but Adams shines as the darkly mysterious and irresistible Octopussy. It's an instant classic.

For starters, she has the coolest pet ever—an extremely venomous yellow and blue octopus that she calls...(wait for it)..."Octopussy." Secondly, she's fabulously wealthy and lives in India in the Floating Palace, where supposedly no men are allowed. Yeah, that rule lasts about thirty seconds with Bond on the case. Finally, and most importantly, she has a cult army. A cult army of beautiful women. Extremely acrobatic and beautiful women. In matching red bodysuits and black bikinis. I'm so jealous.

ERIN: So am I. Also?

HARRY: Yes?

ERIN: Octopussy.

HARRY: Hee.

ERIN: Hee.

Halle Berry as "Giacinta 'Jinx' Johnson" in *Die Another Day*

ERIN: I can't have a top five list without Halle Berry on it. Even if she *weren't* one of the Bond girls, I'd still try to find a way to shove her in here somewhere, because the woman is hotter than the heat of a thousand melting suns. And she was big news even before she agreed to do a Bond movie. Usually, Bond girls are women we've never heard of or established actresses who need a little "push" to their careers. And, no, Berry's not the hottest Girl in the series, because I believe I already mentioned the Famke, no?

HARRY: Yes.

ERIN: The Famke stands. But Berry's Jinx is a hell of a lot smokier than the other Bond girl in the movie, Rosamund Pike, with her pink cheeks and equally pink backstory. Jinx is all sorts of trouble, which you sort of clue into about two seconds after she emerges from the surf in a sexier and oranger version of Honey Ryder's famous bikini. Yeah, her dialogue with Bond is all flirty and entendre-filled and annoying as all get-out, but Berry's pixie cut and molasses-toned curvaceous bod draw your attention away from the stupid talking and put the focus back where it should be: on Berry. You practically forget that Pierce Brosnan's even on the *screen*, let alone in the *room*. I left this movie wondering what kind of damage Halle Berry could do to a female version of the Bond series.

89

HARRY: And then, of course, you saw *Catwoman*....

ERIN: And stopped wondering. At all. Ever.

HARRY: Amen.

Carole Bouquet as "Melina Havelock" in *For Your Eyes Only*

HARRY: While you and I can fundamentally agree that Famke Janssen is brill as Xenia Onatopp, I can't really condone your choice of her as your favorite Bond girl of all time, seeing as she's not officially a Bond girl.

ERIN: I thought I told you—

HARRY: Shhh. It's my turn to talk.

Carole Bouquet, my friend. She's the bomb. She's the bomb because she is truly up against it in this movie. Yes, she appears in the somewhat overlooked *For Your Eyes Only*, a movie that suffers greatly from thoroughly cheesy '80s production values, including glaringly obvious special effects and downright boring chase sequences. Yes, the dialogue is atrocious and the script in general should be taken out back and shot at dawn. And, yes, the other Bond girl in the movie is that dumb-ass tool Bibi Dahl (as played by Lynn-Holly Johnson, who "wowed" us all with her portrayal of a blind figure skater in love with *Robby Benson*—I'm sorry, I think I need to drink a glass of bleach just to get *that* bad taste out of my mouth), who almost manages to single-handedly ruin the Bond girl franchise within the first five minutes she's onscreen. But none of that matters because, as I said, the Bouquet = the Bomb: her beauty is immaculate, she looks fantastic in the totally stupid '80s fashions she's made to wear, she's remarkably intelligent, she has a fabulously untraceable Eurotrash accent that I can't place even to this day, and her favorite accessory is none other than the Big-Ass Crossbow.

Remember that famous poster for the film? The one with the shapely legs that go on for a few billion miles and the spike heels and the barely-there bikini bottom and, of course, that Big-Ass Crossbow? And remember how Bond, framed in the background with his teeny little gun drawn and his teeny little pompadour quivering, appeared almost as an afterthought? Remember how he looked a little intimated by the Big-Ass Crossbow and the Gargantuan Legs of Doom? That poster sealed the deal for me, Bouquet-wise. Yeah, yeah, yeah, those weren't actually her legs. I don't care. It's still a kick-ass poster.

In the end, my love for her might come down to the fact that Melina's not a total slut like most of the Bond girls. Yes, there's the whole "moon-light swim" with Bond at the film's conclusion, but I think she's one of the few Bond girls who didn't just give it up to Bond when he had an itch that needed scratching. Get down with your bad self, sister.

ERIN: You know, I don't think that you can realistically call her a "sister" since you're, you know, a guy.

HARRY: That's not true. The Bond girls transcend time, space, and even gender roles. Melina and I are sisters-in-arms.

ERIN: As long as the arms are Big-Ass Crossbows?

HARRY: Well, *duh*. Also? I think I've figured it out.

ERIN: What?

HARRY: How we Bond fans choose our favorite Bond girls.

ERIN: Oh, this I have to hear.

HARRY: Well, my Bond girls are mostly from 007 films that were contem-porary or shown on network TV when I was a kid. My guess is that my first Bond film was very likely an ABC Sunday Night Movie that stayed on until 10 P.M. and was a full hour past my bedtime. I assume I was so utterly fascinated by this wacky secret agent world that I begged my parents to let me stay up until the end of the movie. So, like my favorite comfort food or Christmas present, my favorite Bond girls occupy a neat little niche of my childhood and adolescence. As an adult, I certainly still enjoy Bond films, but the fascination isn't on the same level. I now see the silliness and plot holes and bad acting and predict the twists well in advance. But they are still a blast.

ERIN: I never thought about it that way. Mostly because I was never into the movies as a kid. My dad loved them, but they're not exactly in a genre that's marketed to young girls, you know? So I didn't get into them until later, when there would be festival showings of them at local theaters and everyone would get drunk and throw stuff at the screen every time Bond lit a cigarette or used a double entendre.

HARRY: Man, you must have been hammered from the first frame.

ERIN: I know, right? But that's what the movies were to me: a good time to be had by all while kind of ignoring the objectification of women or whatever. I never balked at the chicks in bikinis and the seeming irresistibility of Bond no matter how big of a comb-over (Moore? I'm looking directly at you) he was sporting. They were just pure, un-adulterated fun. I didn't start truly enjoying them until later, when they had women in them that were more than just boobs and strate-gically placed weapons. I mean, yeah, they're still all about the boobs and the weapons, but at least now they're also heavily involved in ass-kicking, and some of them are astrophysicists or nuclear weapon engineers....

HARRY: Ahem.

ERIN: ...They're still just bimbos, kind of, aren't they?

HARRY: Uh-huh. But I appreciate where you were going with it. Nice try.

ERIN: Thanks. I was trying to raise the bar here but...no go. The Bond girls are what they are and there's really no way to make them into something that they aren't.

HARRY: Thank God.

And that's the point, really, isn't it? The Bond girls can evolve and change and get prettier and bustier and more competent and less dumb, but they'll always essentially remain the same: hot chicks with guns. And that's why we love them. After all, different Bonds may come and go, but the Bond girl is forever. Forever *hot*, that is. Amen. And hallelujah.

———

In her mind, **ERIN DAILEY** has always been a Bond girl. So if you see her on the street, please refer to her only by her Bond girl name, "Bitchy O'Sarcasm." When she's not wielding weapons while wearing a red snake-skin bodysuit, she manages to cover *Alias* for the Web site Television Without Pity (www.televisionwithoutpity.com). She has contributed articles for the BenBella books *Alias Assumed: Sex, Lies and SD-6* and *Flirting with Pride & Prejudice* and written for such sites as Shebytches (www.shebytches.com) and This Is Not Over (www.thisisnotover.com). She lives and breathes in the jasmine-scented city of Charleston, South Carolina. Catch up with her ramblings at *The Redhead Papers* (www.redhead-papers.com).

In his mind, **HARRY ELLIOTT** has always been a Bond girl. So if you see him on the street, please refer to him only by his Bond girl name, "Dude LooksLikeaLady." Harry works in product development for a "major" dot com. While not making the Internet more user-friendly, Harry thinks of himself as a creative and freelance writer, and has the record for the most single post blogs in history. His latest vaporware may or may not be located at CafeauGay.com. Harry lives and breathes in the exhaust-scented city of Chicago, Illinois, exactly a mile and a half due north of the left-field bleachers of Wrigley Field.

Who Is the Best Bond Villain?

If I Were a Villain, But Then Again, No

I WAS A JAMES BOND nerd when I was a kid. I was around ten years old when the movie *Dr. No* was released in America, and I had read all of the Ian Fleming 007 novels that had been published by that point. My parents didn't seem to mind that I was reading "adult" literature (and in fact, my mother accompanied me to *Dr. No*, the last time I can recall going to the theater with her). For the novels, I started at the beginning, with *Casino Royale*, and have not forgotten to this day the horrible scene where the villain, Le Chiffre, tortures 007 by whacking Bond's testicles with a carpet beater (no less an expert than Raymond Chandler admitted that scene "still haunts me"). It didn't stop me, though, from devouring the rest of the novels, and I jumped at the chance to see Bond on the big screen.

If only that were the extent of my James Bond obsession. But no, I didn't stop there. I had 007 cologne (not sure why I needed this when I was a pre-teen) and a James Bond board game that at least didn't smell bad. I even took to guarding my possessions using a trick I had picked up from a Fleming novel. Before leaving a room, Bond plucked a hair from his head and placed it across a crack in a door. When he returned and the hair was gone, he knew his room had been searched. Being a nerd and not a secret agent, I was far too afraid to pluck out a hair; I used a thread instead.

I wanted to be James Bond. I never wanted to be a villain.

This is only unusual because there have been so many great Bond villains. Auric Goldfinger set the standard for most of what followed. He even got what may still be the most famous one-liner a villain has spouted in any Bond film, when he answered Bond's question, "Do you expect me to talk?" with, "No, Mr. Bond. I expect you to die." But Goldfinger wasn't cool like Bond. A Jack Nicholson might take over a Batman movie, but no one was going to distract us from Sean Connery.

Bond villains are an integral part of what people think of as the classic 007 tradition. No Bond movie could be made without a villain, and often a henchman or two as well. And, of course, two of the first three Bond films were named after their villains. What goes unnoticed, beyond the talk about Goldfinger and Dr. No and Ernst Stavro Blofeld, is how much the villains blend together. The idea of a Bond villain is unavoidable; the reality of the villains, though, is that they are forgotten once each's particular movie has faded into the past. Everyone has their favorite, to be sure, but beyond that, how many people remember the villain in *GoldenEye*? Alec Trevelyan, once known as 006. (More memorable was Xenia Onatopp, played by Famke Janssen, who killed by crushing her opponents between her thighs.) The name Aristotle Kristatos doesn't ring much of a bell (he was the villain in *For Your Eyes Only*). *The Living Daylights*? All you need to know is that he was played by Joe Don Baker.

The point is that the category of the Bond villain has become more important than the actual villains. I would argue that there are only four Bond villains of note: Dr. No, Auric Goldfinger, Ernst Stavro Blofeld, and whoever you liked enough to make number four. (There have also been memorable henchmen; besides the aforementioned Onatopp, one could add Oddjob and Jaws, along with one other I will discuss shortly.)

No particular pattern was set in the first movies. Dr. No does not even appear in his own film until less than half an hour remains. No is a megalomaniac with designs, one suspects, on taking over the world, but his particular job during the film is only to mess with the missiles of the United States for SPECTRE. But Dr. No does not stick in the mind with the lasting power of an Ursula Andress, the first of the Bond girls and in many eyes still the best. He is the first villain, he suggests the direction of future villains, but he is not the final prototype.

From Russia With Love essentially dismissed the notion of a master villain, even though it was the film that introduced Ernst Stavro Blofeld and his omnipresent cat. The real villains in this movie are underlings working for SPECTRE. Robert Shaw's Red Grant gets into a memorable fight with Bond, and the legendary Lotte Lenya wore a famous pair of knife-wielding shoes as Rosa Klebb.

At this point, the Bond movies were following the plot of the novels with relative fidelity, and the idea of a "Bond villain" had yet to be clearly established. With the subsequent *Goldfinger*, new patterns were set in motion. Auric Goldfinger remains to this day the ultimate Bond villain: he is present throughout the film, he has several key scenes with Bond, and he has a plan to take over the world.

Goldfinger is the first movie villain to be working essentially on his own. He has ties to the Chinese, but the primary purpose of his "Operation Grandslam" is to make himself the richest man in the world. (At one point, Goldfinger murders pretty much every mob boss in the United States—not, like Michael Corleone, to clear the way for his own ascension, but merely because they have already served their purpose to Goldfinger.)

Goldfinger is also larger than life, not just in the physical sense (actor Gert Frobe is a big man), but in his ambitions. In the end, Dr. No was just doing SPECTRE's bidding, but Goldfinger? He wanted to set a world record of infamy. "Man has climbed Mount Everest, gone to the bottom of the ocean. He's fired rockets at the moon, split the atom, achieved miracles in every field of human endeavor...except crime!"

And throughout the film, Goldfinger and Bond play cat and mouse, alternating roles. Bond is a good opponent for Goldfinger, a way to put a finishing touch to his criminal miracles. And Goldfinger, of course, is a challenging opponent for Bond as well, and never more so than when he directs the laser toward 007's crotch.

And then there is Blofeld. Goldfinger may be the Übervillain, but Blofeld is the most famous villain, among other things the clearest model for Dr. Evil in the Austin Powers films. Blofeld is the one supporting character to appear in multiple films. As the leader of SPECTRE, he makes brief appearances in *From Russia With Love* and *Thunderball*, before finally showing his face in *You Only Live Twice*. In that film, Donald Pleasence as Blofeld gave Mike Myers a lifetime supply of Evil. Blofeld's plan, backed by the Chinese but of clear benefit to SPECTRE as well, is to start a nuclear war between the U.S. and U.S.S.R. in order to wipe them off the face of the earth. This rather imaginative idea is foiled by 007, of course, but Blofeld escapes to return in several more films. Telly Savalas takes over the role for *On Her Majesty's Secret Service*, committing one of the truly savage acts in any Bond movie when he has Bond's wife murdered. Charles Gray gets the acting job for *Diamonds Are Forever*, which begins with Bond getting his revenge by killing Blofeld, only to find that he's killed a clone instead. Blofeld's ultimate demise is assumed at the end of the film, but the man had as many lives as his ever-present pet cat. Finally, in the pre-credit sequence of *For Your Eyes Only*, Bond dispatches Blofeld for good.

Blofeld's longevity makes him a candidate for the ultimate Bond villain, but I would argue that outside of his responsibility in killing Mrs. Bond, Blofeld is not the most interesting of bad guys. In three of his movies, he makes only brief appearances. In every case, he is played by a different actor, which detracts from whatever continuity his longevity offers. For a while in the later Sean Connery films, Blofeld seemed to be everywhere, but outside of his role in George Lazenby's *On Her Majesty's Secret Service*, in forty-four years he has only made one pre-credit appearance in a non-Connery Bond film. He certainly belongs in the pantheon of Bond villains; he is far from anonymous. But neither is he Goldfinger.

And so we come to my choice for the "fourth Bond villain." But first, it's worth stopping for a moment and imagining how 007 might have appeared to someone who had been with the series from the start. I can only speak to my own experiences. For a child in the '60s, James Bond was a fantasy role model. For a young married adult in the '70s, James Bond was a campy reminder of my youth. But by 1983, James Bond was an object of ridicule. Roger Moore had never been much good in the role, and his Bond films were becoming increasingly worse. Popular culture had taken some interesting turns as well. If Bond, in 1964's *Goldfinger*, felt that listening to the Beatles required earmuffs, one can only guess what he would have thought of punk rock. A thirty-year-old man who had grown up on James Bond would, by 1983, have moved on. It is hard to picture anything 007 could do at that point to get the attention of those old fans.

Enter—or rather, reenter—Sean Connery.

Thanks to a complicated, even confusing, series of arguments and legal rulings over many years, Ian Fleming's novel *Thunderball* was an item of contention, much of it surrounding a man named Kevin McClory, who had a hand in the writing of the novel and managed to procure the film rights to the book. The original *Thunderball* film was made with McClory's participation, but under the aegis of the Broccoli and Saltzman team that had put together the first three pictures. Afterward, McClory kept the film rights, and a decade later, several years into Roger Moore's reign as 007, McClory worked with Connery on a new Bond picture. Various legal problems prevented anything concrete until 1983, when Sean Connery returned to the role of James Bond in a "non-canonical" Bond film, *Never Say Never Again*—essentially a remake of *Thunderball*.

This movie had several things going for it, not least the return of Connery. It was directed by Irvin Kershner, who had worked with Connery in the '60s and whose most recent film had been *The Empire Strikes Back*. The screenplay was by Lorenzo Semple, Jr., who had scripted such strong films as *Pretty Poison* and *Three Days of the Condor* (although more recently, he had worked on movies like the *King Kong* remake and the 1980 *Flash Gordon*). The cast included the legendary Max von Sydow as Blofeld (who wasn't dead in this particular Bond world), lovely Bond girls Barbara Carrera and Kim Basinger, and even a black Felix Leiter in ex-football player Bernie Casey.

And while it is hardly fair to say the film flopped at the box office when it took in $160 million worldwide, nonetheless *Octopussy*, a Roger Moore Bond film released the same year, did better.

What *Never Say Never Again* had that no other 007 film could match was the Austrian actor Klaus Maria Brandauer, fresh off *Mephisto*, which won the Best Foreign Language Oscar in 1982. Playing Blofeld's number two, Maximillian Largo, Brandauer became my own personal Fourth Bond villain. I am admittedly cheating here; if Blofeld is a Bond villain, wouldn't Largo be merely a henchman? But in this film, and indeed in the original *Thunderball*, Blofeld serves no real purpose beyond setting Largo on his assignment.

In the original, Largo is played by Italian actor Adolfo Celi, whose voice was dubbed over. The most memorable aspect of Celi's performance is the eyepatch he wears (Bosley Crowther's rave review in the *New York Times* devoted exactly one sentence to Celi, whom he called "piratical").

Brandauer plays against the stereotype of the Bond villain, which already makes him intriguing. He waltzes through the film like a modern European dandy. He couldn't be further from Celi; an eyepatch would have been an abomination on Brandauer's Largo, who drapes the sleeves of his stylish sweaters over his shoulders.

At one point, he loses a game to Bond, a game Largo himself designed called "Domination." "My problem," he notes, "is I've never yet found a worthy adversary." Until 007, of course. The loser of the game suffers a series of shocks that come through the joysticks the players use. After Largo loses, he doesn't go into a rage; he doesn't order his henchmen to rough up Bond. Instead, he looks at one of his hands, still hurting from the electric volts, and blows it gently, simultaneously cooling it off and delivering Bond's victory into fairy dust.

Nor does Brandauer's Largo dismiss Bond, who he recognizes is indeed a worthy opponent. At one point in *Goldfinger*, 007 tosses off a trademark *bon mot*, to which Goldfinger replies, "Choose your next witticism carefully, Mr. Bond, it may be your last." But in *Never Say Never Again*, when Bond says something equally witty to Largo, Brandauer says "Oh," then laughs and finishes with "Mr. Bond!" At such times, Brandauer is closer to a Bond girl than a Bond villain ("Oh, James!" being a standard piece of Bond girl dialogue), but Brandauer doesn't come across as effeminate, just cultured. Rather like James Bond himself.

As the film progresses, it's hard not to imagine Brandauer in the hero's role. Connery's return is decent enough; he's in great shape, and the maturity of his passing years fits well with his performance. But Brandauer is like a better, blonder Roger Moore, or even, to project forward in time, Pierce Brosnan, and his presence works off Connery's, gives us the opportunity to simultaneously examine the original and a rather kinky alternate version, one that is just as suave and witty and worldly as Connery, but off-kilter enough to suggest new possibilities for the character of 007.

My argument isn't that Brandauer's Largo is just another version of Bond. The differences are ultimately too great. But over time, Bond movies have become a bit ossified. Roger Moore is more lightweight than Sean Connery, Timothy Dalton is darker, Pierce Brosnan is Connery-lite, but in the end, they're all recognizably the same old James Bond. Even George Lazenby fills the bill. Eventually, we forget that there might have been other ways to look at Bond; Brandauer-as-Largo offers one of those other ways. (Given the rather vocal opposition to the choice of Daniel Craig, exemplified in the Web site CraigNotBond.com, I am perhaps merely expressing my own preference here for a new version of James Bond. At the least, I must doubt that such hardcore Internet Bond fans would agree with me that Brandauer's Largo would have made an interesting 007.)

There is, of course, one major problem with Largo-as-Bond: Largo, like the vast majority of Bond villains, is insane. Even here, though, Brandauer manages to pull off a lovely urbane nuttiness, never more obvious than when Kim Basinger's Domino calls Largo crazy and Brandauer replies by gazing oddly at her and saying, "Yeah...maybe. I'm crazy," as if he hadn't really thought about it before, but she was probably right.

There are many Bond villains with a veneer of mannered urbanity; it's a fairly standard scene to have the villain invite Bond to dinner, where their polite conversation is filled with undertones of "I'm going to destroy the world," "No, you are not." Eventually, these villains always lose their cool. But Largo only loses his cool once, when he sees Bond and Domino kissing and he goes into a jealous rage. He is just as interested in causing world unrest as any villain, and he takes the Revenge aspect of SPECTRE very seriously, as he demonstrates when he leaves Domino to be sold as a slave. But even then, he kisses her off with an attitude that seems to say, "Oh, that it weren't so."

Most, if not all, of this is attributable to the acting of Klaus Maria Brandauer. As Roger Ebert noted at the time, Brandauer brings a human element to the film...he is never merely a cartoon. Nor is he slumming, the way some actors will do when they feel a role is beneath them. Brandauer isn't camping up his Largo as a lark; he is giving Largo depth. He is, in short, treating Largo as a legitimate acting job, and applying his considerable acting skills to that job. In the process, he makes his Bond villain stand out from the ultimate facelessness of his counterparts in other 007 movies.

I've spent an awful lot of time making a case for Klaus Maria Brandauer's performance of Largo, considering that I started by claiming there were only three notable Bond villains (none of them Largo), and that all of the rest, no matter how interesting they seemed at first glance, eventually fade in our memories. But one must move beyond that which is easiest. James Bond always took on the greatest villainy; if I am to honor my childhood fantasy of being like James Bond, I, too, need to reach for the more difficult task. Dr. No may have set the villainous world on its path; Ernst Stavro Blofeld may have stuck around the longest; Auric Goldfinger most certainly was the greatest Bond villain of them all (he is the "easiest" choice). But I like to think James Bond would approve of my decision to promote Brandauer's Largo. *Never Say Never Again* is the forgotten stepchild of Bond movies, lumped in with the '60s parody *Casino Royale* as "non-canonical," less popular at the time than the concurrent Roger Moore release, unappreciated compared to the first batch of Connery films. As such, one might imagine the creators of *Never Say Never Again* started with the idea that they would make something of their outsider status. If that is true, then they failed; their movie isn't very different from the canon, after all. As Michael G. Wilson, a Bond producer, has said, "We always start out trying to make another *From Russia with Love* and end up with another *Thunderball*" (which carries special irony given the origins of *Never Say Never Again*). The one thing that actually makes *Never Say Never Again* something different is Klaus Maria Brandauer. If I had seen that film back when I was a nerd, perhaps I would have wanted to be a villain after all.

STEVEN RUBIO teaches writing and critical thinking at American River College. He has previously written on Andy Sipowicz and King Kong for the Smart Pop series. He no longer wishes he was a character in the James Bond universe.

References

Crowther, Bosley. "Screen: 007's Underwater Adventures: Connery Plays Bond in 'Thunderball'." *New York Times*. 22 Dec. 1965. <http://movies2.nytimes. com/mem/movies/review.html?_r=1&title1=&title2=Thunderball%20%28 Movie%29&reviewer=BOSLEY%20CROWTHER&v_id=49850&partner=R otten%20Tomatoes&oref=slogin>.

Wilson, Michael G. "From Russia With Love." *Wikipedia*. 4 Apr. 2006. <http:// en.wikipedia.org/wiki/From_Russia_with_Love>.

Who Is the Best James Bond?

Dalton's Gang
A Fleming Fan Praises
the Best Bond

I CAN KICK JAMES BOND'S ass.

I mean, I can *totally* kick his ass.

According to the SMERSH file referred to in Fleming's novel *From Russia With Love*, Bond (the *book* Bond, natch) is six feet tall and 167 pounds. Bond is scrawny. Like... Adrien Brody scrawny. Like... scrawny as the pretentious "collage artist" who sulks at the end of the bar on Goth Night, hunched over his Midori that he pretends is absinthe because it's sort of the right color, and who goes on about how much cooler Lacuna Coil was "before they sold out" as he absently wonders if he should have more detail added to his coi fish tattoo. No wonder Bond loves that Beretta that Major Boothroyd (both the real person and the character Fleming named after him) dismissively called "a lady's gun" in *Dr. No* (both the book and the film): Bond's skinny little Hilary Duff-y wrists can probably only handle the trigger weight of a Beretta.

I'm an inch and a half shorter than Bond and weigh two hundred pounds. I'm pretty sure I can kick Bond's ass.

Yeah, that SMERSH file also mentions that Bond is good at boxing, knife throwing, and knows a few judo holds. "He looks like a nasty customer," says one Commie SMERSH pinko official, looking at Bond's file photo. But if you dig through the novels, you'll find references to Bond smoking *sixty* cigarettes a day. On average. In *Casino Royale*, Bond smoked *seventy* cigarettes in one day. Get your brain around that. Let's take a typical day for Bond. Over the course of maybe fifteen waking hours, that's *four* coffin nails Bond sucks down every hour. And no smokes with diapers for Mr. Bond. No, siree. Which means that's one unfiltered gasper of specially blended Turkish tobacco (Bond hates Virginia blends, unless he's featured in the film version of *Moonraker*, with its multiple Marlboro product placements) every fifteen minutes. Let's say it takes, I dunno, five minutes to smoke a cigarette. That leaves only forty minutes out of each hour that Bond doesn't have tarry clouds of carcinogens in his chest. Each day Bond has, for 300 minutes—about the running time of a typical Peter Jackson Director's Cut—breath-bags full of poison.

Shall we review? Bond is six feet tall, with a build like Kate Moss. Or maybe Beck, if we're being generous. And he inhales so much freakin' mouth smog, it's a wonder that Quarrel didn't have to add nicotine to Bond's scuba tank mix in *Live and Let Die* (the book, that is) when Bond did that underwater assault/infiltration against Mr. Big on the Isle of Surprise. I don't think it would take much for any reasonably healthy guy to beat up Bond without breaking a sweat. Or, for that matter, any reasonably healthy member of the Tri-Delts without breaking a Revlon's-Sun-Goddess-Pink-lacquered nail. Blofeld, or somebody, during his "Gloating-At-The-Start-Of-The-Third-Act" speech should really say: "I could shoot you right now, Mr. Bond! But no! There's a *better* way! I'm gonna drag you behind the tetherball court and take your lunch money!"

So...if I think old "Wheezy" Bond is such a pushover, why is James Bond—the *book* Bond—such a pivotal icon of my personal pop culture mythology, right up there with Batman and Godzilla? For the record, kiddies...yeah, I'm one of those Fleming "The-Books-Are-Way-Better-Than-The-Movies" snobs, even though I do enjoy the movies a lot. For me, what makes a Bond movie good is how well it keeps true to the spirit of Fleming's books, to say nothing of the plots. *From Russia With Love* is a pretty phenomenal movie that follows the spirit and the plot of a phenomenal novel (despite the sort of clumsy device of having SPECTRE, not SMERSH, pulling the strings behind the conspiracy to humiliate and destroy Bond). Think about it...any novel that JFK loved, especially one that makes deadly and ironic use of his girlfriend Marilyn Monroe's mouth—a mouth that he kissed, fer chrissakes!—has got to be pretty freakin' good, huh? And it's pretty amazing that the film could tap the book's power and spirit. That keeping-true-to-Fleming's-spirit requires a certain infusion of *depth*, and I know there's some fancy-schmancy reader of New York trendoid trust-funder literature (read: "pastiche parading as postmodern") out there rolling his/her eyes through a fog of patchouli as he/she *tsk!*s over his/her vanilla soy foam vegan decaf latte at the thought of a Bond narrative having depth. To you, I say—read *Casino Royale*, and if you find that it's not one of the most exquisitely bleak expressions of post-WWII moral isolation, on a par with the best of Chandler, well...just light up another clove cigarette and wait for the next book to come out from a Bennington grad, Poopsie.

The depth of great Bond narratives, in film and in print—a depth comparable to that of the aforementioned Raymond Chandler's Phil Marlowe stories—is based upon Bond's personal sense of duty and honor (and it speaks volumes that Fleming and Chandler were pals). The world of Fleming's Cold War, rather like Chandler's Los Angeles, is a rotten and amoral place, as existentially alienating as anything Camus imagined. Chandler's Los Angeles can be thought of as a character in the Marlowe stories, maybe as a sort of moral inversion—a doppelganger—of Marlowe himself. Maybe, not to belabor the homophonic point, you could say that Los Angeles is as much Marlowe's doppelganger as Mr. Kurtz was that of Conrad's Marlow in *Heart of Darkness*. I'd argue that only a world as morally alienating as Fleming's vision of the Cold War could allow for the incredible sense of existential *danger* that Fleming infused into the climaxes of his novels, to the point that even sensible readers can keep the window of disbelief open for some of Fleming's more absurd conceits, such as Dr. No having a captive giant squid handy as an implement of torture and murder.

Fleming's Cold War, as a character lurking in the background, as malignant and aware a motivating force as Blofeld himself was in the novel *Thunderball*, is Bond's doppelganger. It's a shitty world in which great and wonderful guys like former circus strongman and raw-food aficionado Kerim Bey can survive a bomb blast only to die like a bitch at the hands of Red Grant, women like Mrs. Krest can be flogged with a stingray tail, and girls like Tiffany Case can be gang raped as teenagers. It's a world in which your best pal can be fed to the sharks by *Live and Let Die*'s Mr. Big, or be incinerated by Dr. No's mechanical "dragon." It's a world in which a girl like Vesper Lynd...well...let's not talk about Vesper, shall we? Or for that matter, the late Mrs. Tracy Bond?

The Cold War is Bond's deadly "other," and it manifests itself as the inverse of those virtues that define Bond's moral universe. *Moonraker*'s Hugo Drax is a pus-filled rotter, and his rottenness isn't so much defined by the fact that he's building a rocket that will kill hundreds of thousands, but by the fact that he (*Shudder!*) cheats at cards at the Blades Club, grinning and braying through his crooked ogre's teeth—one of the most tasteless displays at the venerable Club until Madonna showed up there in fencing gear. Goldfinger cheats at cards and golf, and it's hugely telling that the centerpiece of the novel *Goldfinger* isn't some dorky chase scene like the ones that stop the film *Diamonds Are Forever* dead (c'mon...a freakin' *Moon Buggy chase* through the Nevada desert?), but the psychological warfare waged between Bond and Goldfinger on the greens. The central moment of *Diamonds* the novel is when Bond witnesses the cruelty of the smugglers as they rough up innocent bystanders at Acme Mud and Sulphur. Yeah, these guys, the Spangled Mob, are dirty rotten crooks, but Bond truly wants to stop them because they're bullies.

The depth of Bond, of both the character and the narratives centered around that character, lies in the fact that Bond, to crib from *Hamlet*, is to his own self true, a quality he shares with Marlowe. This is not a quality that makes him irresistible to women, one of the most defining aspects of the filmic Bond and one that has proven to be such a gleeful object of parody in the Austin Powers movies. It's a quality that makes Bond's ideals and codes of ethics irresistible to him. Let me give you an example of this in the context of a body of Bond work that I'm really not crazy about, but that was so cool for a guy with a paradigm of Bond fandom like mine that it's worth mentioning here, because it gleams so dramatically against a background of general mediocrity. Roger Moore is my least favorite Bond.[1] But after the bloated excesses of the film version of *Moonraker*, it was a joy in *For Your Eyes Only* to see Moore play a Bond with the kind of haunted depth I describe above. This may be the reason that Leonard Maltin saw fit to write of *For Your Eyes Only*: "No other James Bond film has provoked so much debate among 007 fans...." I'm one of those Bond fans who thought it was brilliant and satisfying to see Moore as Bond kick that murdering bastard Locque over a cliff after Locque killed MI6 agent Ferarra and Countess Lisl (played by the now-late wife of Pierce Brosnan, Cassandra Harris). The last killer with no dialogue we'd had in a Bond film up to that point had been the utterly cartoonish Jaws, who became a good guy when the plot of *Moonraker* necessitated it. In *For Your Eyes Only*, the silent killer was a truly ruthless prick who seemed to enjoy his work.

Only a Bond who is haunted, who like Marlowe has an evil opposite in the form of the monstrously bleak world he inhabits, could off Locque and make the act satisfying for both Bond and the audience. At the end of the

---

[1] Yes, he's waaaaay behind Lazenby, in my book. *On Her Majesty's Secret Service* is a righteously cool Bond movie, one of the best. See it again, if you don't believe me. It might just be the only Bond movie to improve on the Fleming work on which it is based.

aforementioned movie version of *Moonraker*, Moore's Bond pumps Drax full of cyanide and blasts him out of an airlock, quipping: "Take a giant step back for mankind." That's a stunningly horrible death, but it didn't shock anybody the way that Moore's kicking Locque over that cliff did. That's because there was no depth to *Moonraker*. It was an expression of the Banal Bond, who operates only on a surface level—who doesn't exist in a world of dark existential cruelty but a world of shiny buttons and gadgets. Hell, in Moore's first foray into Bond-om, he shoved compressed air down Kananga's throat until the man burst, albeit cartoonishly. Just how many bullets did Moore pump into Karl Stromberg's chest at the end of *The Spy Who Loved Me*? Was it the violence of Locque's death that freaked out some Bond fans, or was it the *context*? A context in keeping with Fleming's dark and deadly vision of the world?

And I wanna point out that by "banal," I don't mean in the strict dictionary definition of "dull and ordinary." Such a use of the term would be...well...banal. In this context, I mean a much more dynamic (if such a modifier can be applied) idea. The banality I speak of is an aggressive and active vapidity that has the implication of making culture itself hollow and unsatisfying as a really stale and waxy Chocolate Easter Bunny. Yeah, that initial biting off of the ears might be fun, but once you hit where that bunny brain oughta be, it tastes really bad and makes your teeth hurt. In this post–Hannah Arendt world, in which she had famously described the captured Nazi Eichmann in terms of "the banality of evil," the word "banal" has gone far beyond being just a thesaurus entry for "boring" or "workaday"; the implication can, in certain discourses, refer to a certain eroding kind of absence.[2]

So there's Banal Bond, and then there's Book Bond, to whom he stands opposite. And in my humble but unimpeachable opinion, movie incarnations of Bond avoid banality when the good folks at EON Productions allow the qualities of the Book Bond to shine through: his non-campy patriotism (expressed through his actions, not Union Jack parachutes), his loyalty to his friends, his sense of justice, and his perseverance. Let's consider his perseverance for a moment in the novel *Moonraker*. No quips could be made while Bond willfully put his own face in an open fire source to save Gala Brand, only to be ditched by her and left alone on a park bench like Jethro Tull's Aqualung.

And what are the qualities that define the Banal Bond? What is the so-

---

[2] It's sort of interesting in this context that Bond and M, in the novel *On Her Majesty's Secret Service*, talk about "doing a kidnap job" on Blofeld, "rather like the Israelis did with Eichmann."

ASK DR. YES

Dear Dr. Yes,

James Bond slept with my sister and now she's dead, covered in a layer of gold. I tried to kill her murderer, unsuccessfully? I met Bond and he didn't even try to sleep with me. I mean, what's that about? I'm at least as hot as my sister.

Anyway, here's my question. I estimate there's about 100 ounces of gold covering my sister, with a market value of over $30,000. Any suggestions as to how to get this gold off? I'll be damned if I'm burying it with her.

Sincerely,
The Good-looking Sister

Dear Good-looking,

How callous can you be? Has it ever occurred to you that James was still heartbroken over the death of your sister? It sometimes takes him days to get over it when a lover dies due to thoughtless actions on his part. Plus, you aren't all that good-looking, frankly.

Regarding your poor sister, I know just what to do. The exact same thing happened to an aunt of mine. Ship the body to me and I'll take care of every-thing.

Sincerely,
Dr. Yes

ciocultural context of that banality? When Bond is banal, the banality is the same as that of *The Flintstones* and *The Jetsons*.

Yes, go back and reread that last sentence.

Yes, I really did say that.

I bet you're saying right now: "Boy! Mike must be smoking somethin' really good! I wished he'd share!"

But think about it, Padawan. What was the main thread of humor throughout both *The Flintstones* and *The Jetsons*? What was its historical context? In postwar consumerist society, there was an explosion of commodities infiltrating homes. This was a life-changing trend, as Betty

Friedan mentioned in *The Feminine Mystique*: "The suburban housewife—she was the dream image of young American women and the envy, it was said, of women all over the world. The American housewife—freed by science and labor-saving appliances from the drudgery, the dangers of childbirth, and the illnesses of her grandmother."

This didn't create so much culture shock, as, perhaps, consumer shock. The humor of *The Flintstones*, with its primitive animal-powered appliances, and of *The Jetsons*, with its absurdly high-tech fetishization of convenience (to the point of living rooms having moving sidewalks), is a hyperbolizing of the changes that gadgets wrought upon daily life.

This Western, postwar consumerist fetishization and hyperbolizing of gadgetry is shifted from the realm of Levittown living rooms to the realm of Cold War not-so-*realpolitik* in the Bond films. Yeah, Le Chiffre's tricked-out car was a kind of gadget in the novel *Casino Royale*, but it was a deadly gadget that just about any really good machinist could rig up. It doesn't rate on the same gadget-y scale as, say, Bond's amphibious Lotus in the movie *The Spy Who Loved Me*. That Lotus (welcomely blown to scrap in *For Your Eyes Only*) and his freakin' amphibious gondola in *Moonraker* (and I thought *Diamond*'s Moon Buggy was a buzzkill), as gadgets, push the same cultural buttons as do the gadgets of *The Flintstones* and *The Jetsons* (though, on *The Flintstones*, a true amphibian would be the motivating force behind the gadget/commodity/appliance). Bond's gondola, Wilma's mastodon-nosed dishwasher, and the Jetson's treadmill dogwalker all occupy the same cultural niche of banality. There's a reason why Bondian gadgets could be featured in the flick *A Man Called Flintstone*, if you think about it.

Bond's strength as a character, in the novels and in the best of the films, transcends his scrawny, cancer-lunged physical presence, with its dainty Julia Roberts-y wrists that so favor the trigger pull of a totally girly Beretta. His strength as a character transcends that banalizing influence, gadget fetishization, and hyperbole. What makes Bond a brilliant, driving cultural force is his opposition to his doppelganger and his "other": the gravitas he gains as the exact inversion of the rotten world of the Cold War, either as that Cold War world exists in fact, or in his own perceptions.

These strengths have been given their best expression to date in the performances of Timothy Dalton as Bond. Yes, I'm putting into a larger sociocultural context what is essentially the assertion of a girlfriend-less fanboy, typed out with orange Dorito-stained fingertips on an Internet message board between sips of flat, room-temperature Jolt Cola: "Dude! Dalton...like...totally RAWKS!" But acting, like writing, painting, or any other art form, is influenced by, and can be a comment upon, sociocultural forces and contexts. More than any other actor (as of this writing Daniel Craig is still filming *Casino Royale*), Dalton, while playing an iconic role, had the skill and talent to integrate the qualities of the Book Bond into the screen persona of Bond, in a manner that nearly erased all traces of the Banal Bond. Dalton's Bond, at the historic moment of the late 1980s when *The Living Daylights* (1987) and *Licence to Kill* (1989) were released, tapped then-current sociocultural trends in a way that allowed the spirit of Fleming's Cold War–hardened Bond of thirty years previous to be recontextualized in a world in which the Cold War was ending. By being true to the Bond defined by conflict with the Soviets, Dalton's interpretation of Bond allowed the character to survive as a vibrant cultural force after the fall of the Soviet Union. Dalton's Bond is a man defined by his own integrity, which in turn is defined as the inverse of the morally rotten world of the Cold War. Dalton's Bond is so thoroughly and perfectly defined by that "other" that his Bond, haunted by that doppelganger, functions in a non–Cold War narrative as no banal Bond possibly could. Dalton's Bond is so thoroughly an echo of the Book Bond, so thoroughly defined by the soul-killingly bleak Cold War world articulated by Fleming, that his Bond can function without the "training wheels" of a strictly Cold War narrative and setting, rather like how Fleming's Bond can function in the novel *The Spy Who Loved Me* without the "training wheels" of a Cold War conflict (even though the backstory deals with Bond's hunting SPECTRE agents in North America).[3]

An elegant expression of this can be found in the non-Cold War *Licence to Kill*, in which Dalton's Bond whacks a henchman of Milton Krest, who has killed Bond's friend, Sharkey (who, for all intents and purposes, is an iteration of Quarrel, following the film series' Quarrel of *Dr. No* and Quarrel, Jr., of *Live and Let Die*). As the henchman pulls up Sharkey's boat along Krest's, he delights in telling Krest, as Sharkey is strung up alongside the sharks he had been catching as a cover while helping Bond infiltrate Krest's operation, Sharkey's name. Bond avenges his friend. It's *personal* as he kills the henchman with a spear-gun, saying coldly: "Compliments of Sharkey!" It's a violent and brutal act that is appropriate and right in a violent and brutal world. Dalton's Bond uses violence and he *means* it. The violence

---

[3] And yes, as a Fleming fan, it's hard for me to defend the truly appalling 1962 novel *The Spy Who Loved Me* (the main plot of which concerns Bond stumbling across petty gangsters in upstate New York) as anything really worth reading beyond a curiosity piece. In terms of cultural history, it's interesting to think of the novel's narrator, twenty-three-year-old Vivienne Michel, as a young woman coming of age throughout the '60s. She's the exact same age as Mary Tyler Moore's signature character Mary Richards (she'd be around thirty in 1970). How did Women's Lib affect the rather flighty Vivienne, who so thoroughly fell for her rescuer? Food for thought. . . .

itself has meaning, rather like the moment in which Moore's Bond kicked Locque over the cliff, because the act is that of a man haunted by his doppelganger, the rotten world of the Cold War that Fleming articulated.

Compare Dalton's sincere killing of Krest's henchman with the moment in *Thunderball* when Connery's Bond offs a guy with a spear-gun, an act that was a joke, punctuated by the punchline, "I think he got the point!" The jokiness of Connery's quip makes the killing morally safe, divorcing and distancing Bond's acts of violence from the existentially bleak world of Fleming's imagination and freeing the character of Bond from that bleak world. We in the audience are let off the hook; the joke expiates us. It's indicative of the larger shift to banality begun in *Thunderball* and continued though the series' devolution throughout the late '60s to the mid-'80s, with respites coming in the form of *On Her Majesty's Secret Service* and *For Your Eyes Only*. This distancing from bleakness and softening of brutality makes Bond a creature of surface gloss and gadgets, a character who can't confront brutal villains because he himself is not capable of (warranted) brutality in return.

True, Dalton had his share of quips, but they were not delivered as jokes. Toward the end of *The Living Daylights*, after Bond killed the not-so-subtly-named assassin Necros by cutting the laces of the boot to which Necros clung as both Bond and Necros dangled from the end of a Hercules aircraft, Dalton's Bond mutters, "He got the boot!" But Dalton's delivery is one of bitter irony, a comment on the arbitrary and cruel nature of the world he inhabits, and by which he is haunted.

There's another fine moment in *Licence to Kill*, in which Bond stuffs an unconscious guy into an incubator drawer full of maggots, softly saying to the worms, "Bon appetit!" This is a moment of darkness too severe for any previous Bond to have pulled off with the seriousness with which Dalton does. Roger Moore, in contrast, can off Tee Hee, Kananga's one-armed henchman, and call the encounter "disarming." Such light-heartedness is impossible with Dalton's Bond, which is not to say that Dalton is incapable of humor and spoof; look to his Errol Flynn parody in *The Rocketeer* and his turn as Bond caricature Damien Drake in *Looney Tunes, Back in Action*. Yet even Connery in his most lethal moments could not have pulled off the hotel room invasion of *The Living Daylights*, in which Dalton's Bond terrorized General Pushkin and his mistress. The entire scene, crucial to the plot, only works if the audience is convinced of Bond's intent, or at least his capability, of executing Pushkin, and that such a killing would have dire consequences that couldn't be "disarmed" with a quip.

I mentioned how an artist can tap sociocultural forces in the creation of his or her work. What sociocultural forces did Dalton tap in the creation of his uniquely lethal Bond? (Which is not to say he created his Bond without the help of director John Glen and screenwriters Michael G. Wilson and Richard Maibaum.) Let's consider the historic context in which Dalton created his Bond, with the advantage of almost twenty years' hindsight: the late 1980s climax of the Cold War. It's telling that 1977's *The Spy Who Loved Me*, made while Carter was in office but before the Soviet invasion of Afghanistan and the subsequent U.S. boycott of the 1980 Summer Olympics, was rife with the spirit of détente, with Bond teaming up with Soviet spy Major Anya Amasova to bring down Stromberg, a villain who did for supertankers and subs what SPECTRE did for spacecraft. By 1981's *For Your Eyes Only*, Bond-ian détente entailed Bond smashing the McGuffin ATAC device and telling General Gogol: "That's détente, Comrade! You don't have it. I don't have it."

The solidification of Reaganite and Thatcherite political ideologies in the U.S. and the U.K., particularly after the invasions of the Falklands and Grenada, manifested themselves in popular culture in works of great maturity and vapidity. For each facile teen doomsday fantasy like *War Games*, there was *The Day After*, *Threads*, *Special Bulletin*, and *Testament*. With the advent of infantile bolus like *Rambo*, *Red Scorpion* (produced by disgraced lobbyist Jack Abramoff), *Red Dawn*, and *Rocky IV*, there were also the very fine and bleak miniseries versions of John Le Carre's *Smiley's People* and *A Perfect Spy*.

The climax of the Cold War was reflected in these pop culture artifacts, knowingly or not on the part of their creators. The clean-cut All-American teens of *Red Dawn*, crushing the mighty Soviet Army with the help of *deus ex machina* Cheerios, and the exhausted stare of Alec Guinness's Smiley, belong on opposite ends of the same cultural spectrum. The sociocultural trends which gave us a then-thirty-two-year-old Patrick Swayze as a teenage guerrilla and Elie Weisel and Carl Sagan talking about nuclear war after the broadcast of *The Day After* (to say nothing of the Ben Stein–conceived miniseries *Amerika*) could not help but have an impact on the premiere Cold War pop culture meta-narrative that had begun more than twenty years before with the release of *Dr. No*. Physical confrontation with a Cold War superman had meant Connery's Bond fighting to the death with Red Grant (he of the red wine with fish preference) on the Orient Express. In the miasma of the 1980s, such a confrontation meant Rocky Balboa fighting *Rocky IV*'s Ivan Drago (he of the implied steroid use) in a Stalinist arena. After the 1983 placement of Pershing missiles in the U.K. and West Germany, and the subsequent protests from the Campaign for

Nuclear Disarmament, the notion of a "secret missile base" like SPEC-TRE's volcano launch pad in *You Only Live Twice* somehow lost its kitsch value. The world had changed, and the Bond series had to acknowledge this, eschewing vapidity, which had become really vapid, and competing on some level with the works of maturity being produced.

It goes without saying that Bond is the center of the Bond-ian universe. The more depth Bond has, the more depth his world has, and the less it must rely on gadgets, gloss, and shiny surface banality. I mentioned that the non–Banal Bond is defined by his doppelganger: the ugly world of Cold War brutality and moral alienation. Bond the character defines the world that we the audience inhabit while watching Bond films or reading Bond novels. *Licence to Kill*, the Bond film most divorced narratively from the Cold War, dealing as it does with drug trafficking free of the Soviet backing that funded Mr. Big's in the novel *Live and Let Die*, is still the Bond narrative most defined by Bond's personal code, by Bond's "otherness" from the morally alienating Cold War. In most Bond films, Bond is moved into action by M's orders. *Licence to Kill* features a Bond whose motives are entirely his own. And no other actor who has played Bond could carry a film with a narrative and a premise such as that of *Licence to Kill*, because no other actor has allowed his interpretation of Bond to be defined by that haunting "other" of the world of the Cold War to the extent that Dalton has. It is this definition by the "other," the depth and the gravitas of this definition, that allows Bond to define the Bond-ian universe, much more so than Q's handiwork.

While filming *Chimes at Midnight*, Orson Welles said, "The drama itself dictates the kind of world in which it is going to happen." Dalton's Bond, haunted like no other actor's, defined by his world like no other actor's, creates the most compelling drama of the film series. The drama carried by Dalton's Bond in turn infuses the Bond-ian world with a strength and realism that gives the films the kind of boot-to-the-teeth impact that Fleming's books have. It is a Bond-ian universe defined by a mythic Cold War that is strong and compelling enough to transcend the limitations of the real Cold War, which was reaching its climax and ending as the Dalton films were produced. It's what's inside Bond that counts, and what's inside is a toughness that isn't limited by his slight frame and grotesque smoking habits. Dalton's Bond is the truest to Fleming's and, as such, the "character" that is the world he inhabits is the truest and most resonant. A believable world is a world in which we, as an audience, can participate, a world in which we're not let off the hook with a quip-y punch line. Bond has a license to kill, yet Dalton's Bond does not give us, the audience, a license to laugh off those killings. We share his Bond's existential vision, which takes Bond out of the realm of superhero voyeurism and into the world of real conflict. In short...Dalton, my friends, for the true Fleming fan, totally RAWKS.

For the past fifteen years, **MICHAEL MARANO**'s work has appeared on the Public Radio Satellite Network program *Movie Magazine International*, syndicated in more than 111 markets in the U.S. and Canada. His commentary on pop culture has appeared in venues such as *The Boston Phoenix*, *The Independent Weekly*, *The Weekly Dig*, *Science Fiction Universe*, and *Paste* magazine. Marano's short fiction has been published in several high-profile anthologies, including the Lambda-winning Queer Fear series, *The Mammoth Book of Best New Horror 11*, and *Outsiders: 22 All-New Stories from the Edge*; his first novel *Dawn Song* won the Bram Stoker and International Horror Guild Awards.

Eat Like Bond

ANDREA CARLO CAPPI

BOND IS KNOWN for his ability to enter any restaurant in the world and always order the right dish with the right wine (or beer). Here is a short selection of some of Bond's favorite foods.

At the Casino Royale
Bond's dinner in Fleming's novel of the same title includes caviar, *tournedos*—well cooked—with *béarnaise* sauce and a bit of artichoke, and half an avocado *à la français* for dessert. I don't know what most of it means, but according to Fleming it's very good. Champagne is, of course, required.

At Ma Frazier's, in Harlem, New York
In *Live and Let Die* Bond and Leiter have fried chicken with ham and sweet corn (also Billie Holiday's favorite dish, according to her autobiography *Lady Sings the Blues*). No information about drinks, although Bond's favorite drink in New York is usually Miller High Life beer.

At the Blades Club, London
Smoked salmon (from the Highlands, not from Scandinavia), followed by lamb cutlets and asparagus with *hollandaise sauce*, and finished off with a pineapple slice, all with Dom Perignon, since M is paying the bill at his club in the novel *Moonraker*. Although I'd personally suggest a good red wine with the cutlets—not with the salmon.

At Scott's, Near the Old SIS Headquarters

In *Diamonds Are Forever*, the suggestion Bond gives to M's chief of staff Bill Tanner is special crabs with a pint of brown beer. Seafood with brown beer is quite an interesting mix.

In an Italian Restaurant

In the short story "Risico," from the *For Your Eyes Only* collection, Bond has *spaghetti al pesto*, with the typical green sauce made of basil, garlic, and pine nuts. *Pesto* actually originated in the Italian Riviera, and Fleming might have tasted it in the '30s, while following a car race near San Remo. You can have chianti with it, but the best wine suggestion—trust me, I've been there a lot—is a local white wine from the original *pesto* area: vermentino, pigato, or cinque terre.

Wherever

In Fleming's non-fiction book *Thrilling Cities* you can find plenty of food suggestions, but there's also the lesser known bonus short story "007 in New York," where we learn all about Bond's favorite dish: scrambled eggs "James Bond," with butter, salt, pepper, and finely chopped chives or fine herbs. Tattinger pink champagne and low music recommended.

HOW TO MAKE JAMES BOND YOUR BITCH

Chinks in the Armor
James Bond's
Critical Mistakes

AH, THOSE FAMOUS WORDS, that classic introduction: "The name is Bond—James Bond."

We've heard that so often, and isn't it just brilliant? Thank you, 007; you've just saved the bad guys a lot of investigative work. Have you forgotten you're supposed to be a *secret* agent? Really, would it be so very difficult to say, "My name's Fred Jackson," and smile charmingly?

"We" represent a confidential board of review composed of retired operatives and experts in various fields, appointed by Parliament in hopes of improving the Government's performance in certain areas, including clandestine operations. We have been charged with going over the history of Her Majesty's Secret Service, determining what has worked well in the past and what has not, and offering suggestions for improvement.

M has asked us to review your case files, 007, and point out some of your critical mistakes—oh, not the simple, one-time mistakes, the errors in judgment, the instances where you trusted the wrong woman or shot the wrong man, but the recurring themes, the problems that crop up again and again throughout your career. The theory is that making you aware of your flaws will help you lessen them, thereby improving your chances of survival on future missions.

117

Given that you've already survived this long, and that thanks to you we haven't all fallen victim to some madman's scheme for nuclear blackmail or world domination, one could argue that you haven't *made* any critical mistakes, and there's a great deal to be said for that position, but my colleagues and I believe we have identified a few things that might prove critical in the future, and that are certainly areas of concern, with obvious room for improvement.

Your ongoing resistance to actually staying undercover is one of them. Announcing your true identity to anyone you happen to meet at a bar or across a gaming table is really not in accord with policy.

Practice these phrases, 007: "My name isn't Bond." "I don't know what you're talking about." "I was just passing through." "The British Consulate will hear about this!" Try to imagine yourself actually saying them in the field. Oh, we know most of the bad guys won't believe you when you deny your identity, but if you could just learn to act a little you might at least put a bit of doubt into them. Telling everyone who you are may be good for the ego, but it is *not* good for the mission.

Please, stop giving your real name.

There might have been a time when you could justify this little quirk by saying that the name James Bond shouldn't mean anything to your typical world-conquering megalomaniac, it's just a boring, ordinary name, but really, 007, that dog won't hunt anymore. Even if the public at large hasn't seen your name in the newspapers, word gets around. International terrorist organizations, ex-Communist mercenaries, crazed multimillionaires, and the like don't live in a vacuum; they *compare notes*, 007. Surely you realize that. Why build one's world-spanning conspiracy from scratch, reinventing the wheel as it were, when you can learn so much from those who have gone before? Modern megalomaniacs do their best to stay informed and learn from the errors of their predecessors. And guess whose name always comes up?

Yes, word of your identity does get out, despite the devastation you leave in your wake. When you blow up the secret island lair, or the villain disposes of his own men once they're no longer needed, you don't really think *all* the underlings die, do you? Remember just how huge some of those lairs were, and how many hundreds of technicians, scientists, thugs, concubines, advisors, assassins, engineers, torturers, bodyguards, drivers, and assorted other minions it took to run them. Some of those people always survive, if only by sheer dumb luck—the fellow who was out getting coffee and donuts when the balloon went up, the chaps in the blast-proof underground vault, the ones who crawled out of the wreckage miraculously unhurt. No, Felix Leiter and his CIA pals don't always put all of them behind bars.

And it's not as if you do much to help with rounding up the underlings. We know it's not your job, you're there for the big picture, stop the mastermind's evil scheme and you've earned your pay, but *somebody* has to do it. You might want to make some effort to say a few words about that: point the fellows in the right direction, mention where the secret tunnels are. It would make things ever so much easier for the cleanup crew.

So a few underlings survive and slip away before we can incarcerate them. Now, if you're a minion who's escaped from the catastrophic failure of a world-conquering scheme, what sort of job do you find next? What can you put on your resume? You'll hire on with the next megalomaniac who comes along, because that's the only sort of person who'll hire you, and you'll tell him all about that dreadful Mr. James Bond who blew up your last boss, in hopes that maybe this time the scheme will work, the world will stay conquered, and you'll get your little piece of the action.

So please, 007—do try to maintain your cover just a *little* longer, rather than announcing yourself. We know it's hard on your ego, pretending to be someone else when you're so very obviously wonderful as yourself, but *try*.

And speaking of ego, it's not just the name. Would it kill you to drink a martini that had been stirred? Don't you ever feel overdressed, wearing a tuxedo so much of the time? Have you ever considered driving a Toyota rather than a Ferrari, and perhaps obeying the speed limit rather than making every little jaunt look like Le Mans? *Must* you draw attention to yourself at every opportunity? Blending into the crowd really can be useful sometimes. The sheer *gall* you display, your open arrogance, is really rather disconcerting. If we were using you as the diversion while our real master spy slipped into the villain's headquarters unnoticed, that would be one thing, but 007, you *are* the master spy, not the diversion. Making yourself so bloody obvious rather wastes any element of surprise you might have had.

Yes, yes, we know, you're trying to lure the evil mastermind out of hiding by making yourself a target, but one of these days you're going to run into an evil mastermind bright enough to realize it, and he'll either ignore you or kill you in some simple, fairly foolproof way, such as dynamiting your hotel (or better, your girlfriend's hotel), rather than inviting you to dinner, setting up an elaborate deathtrap, or sending exotic assassins after you with rare poisons and razor-edged derby hats.

There are other ways of getting inside the fortress besides being taken in under heavy guard as the mastermind's soon-to-be-murdered guest, you know.

Well, yes, you do know, because often enough you've swum in through a submarine pen or crawled in through an air vent, and in those cases your displays of ego are relatively harmless. They merely ensure that when you're captured, the villain won't need to ask who you are—he'll already know.

Saving the evil mastermind a few minutes of interrogative effort is not really something we want to encourage, 007.

Have you ever considered hiring on as a low-level minion? I mean *really* hiring on, rather than whacking some poor bastard on the head and stealing his uniform half an hour before doomsday. You could infiltrate the evil organization weeks or months in advance, get a look at exactly what it's doing, report back to headquarters on who's been supplying these arch-villains with their hardware, where they're hiring their technicians, all manner of useful little tidbits like that, and *then* take down the megalomaniac and blow up his lair. Maybe then we and the other good guys could make it a little more difficult for the *next* world-conquering crackpot to equip his troops and build his secret headquarters.

Or, just possibly, you might consider *not* blowing up the villain's lair; has it ever occurred to you that some of that stuff might be useful? Not just the information about where the bad guys get all those expensive high-tech toys that you blithely obliterate when you destroy the computer systems, but the toys themselves. That's got to be a few billion pounds of hardware and real estate you've destroyed; it could have been turned over to Her Majesty's government for its own use, or for resale to trusted allies. You know, the British government has no serious qualms about owning orbital death rays, or maintaining secret outposts on uncharted islands; in fact, this sort of thing could be quite handy sometimes. Getting the funding through Parliament could be difficult, and building it ourselves might have the Americans looking askance, but if it just *falls into our lap*, no, we are *not* morally obligated to blow it up.

A good island lair or undersea base or hideout under the polar icecap has many possible uses; it isn't *just* for world domination. A forward listening post here, a covert refueling station there—Britain could *use* these, 007.

Really, destroying them all seems terribly wasteful. Yes, we want them out of the villains' hands, but can't you ever find a way to manage that short of wholesale annihilation?

And of course, you always escape the conflagration at the last minute.

The *last* minute. Might you ever consider setting the timer for a few minutes more, so you can make *sure* the arch-villain and his major henchmen are really dead, and won't be back for a sequel?

It's just sloppy, 007. For someone so fastidious about food, drink, and clothing, you can be astonishingly sloppy about your work. Blown covers, ruined equipment, escaped bad guys, demolished lairs—it's dreadfully untidy.

And then of course, there's that other area where you are noted for being something less than fastidious. Really, 007, must you bed *every* attractive woman you encounter?

Yes, we understand that you have been successful several times in acquiring vital information from your playmates, and sometimes in convincing your foe's female associates to betray their employer and come over to our side, but a little more selectivity might be a good idea. Seducing your CIA counterparts may save on hotel bills, but it does nothing to hasten the successful completion of your assignments, and the benefits in international goodwill are at best trivial and more often nonexistent. Furthermore, involving random strangers in your work simply because they happen to be absurdly attractive is not in keeping with the policies of Her Majesty's government concerning sensitive operations.

And then there's the whole question of being lured into traps by women who were not as thoroughly seduced as you thought. Don't try to tell us it hasn't happened; we've read the files. Admittedly, you've always managed to survive and turn the tables, but it *is* an added risk.

That does not even mention the little detail that the mortality rate among your bed partners is appalling. Getting beautiful women killed is not part of your job, nor do we consider it advisable. It's not as if the world has a huge surplus of them; those of us less favored by Nature than you do not appreciate this reduction in the supply. Yes, it does establish that your opponents are absolute rotters, but honestly, we don't really need that much proof; generally, the construction of a death ray or an attempt at nuclear blackmail is enough to convince us. Leaving a woman dead in your bed and making it personal is unnecessary.

We would never advise you to attempt celibacy; even if we thought you would pay any attention, we don't think it's possible. You wouldn't be *you*, 007, if you didn't have an eye for the ladies. We merely suggest you try to cut back a little and choose your targets more carefully.

Really, 007, that's all we ask—a bit of restraint. Don't be quite so obvious about who you are. Don't be quite so quick to blast everything to smithereens. Don't be quite so eager to tumble into bed. Is that so very difficult?

We can guess how you'll respond, 007. You'll point to your unbroken streak of more than forty years of successfully defeating megalomaniacs and evil international conspiracies, and ask why we want to fix something that isn't broken. We concede you have a point; really, how critical can these flaws be when they haven't resulted in a single failure in so long?

But admit it, 007—you've been lucky. You know it, we know it, everyone knows it. Your enemies have had dozens of opportunities to simply put a bullet in your brain, and as yet they've never actually *done* it. Their compulsion to make speeches and play elaborate games has always saved you.

Sooner or later, though, your luck will run out. You'll find yourself up against a mastermind who puts more faith in a 9mm slug than in an elaborate laser deathtrap, who considers a knife in the belly more efficient than an exotic Oriental assassin's projectiles and poisons, and who really isn't interested in games or speeches. When that happens, the mistakes we have pointed out here really *may* be critical. They may well be what get you killed. Your forty-year streak of luck may not last forever.

Which brings us to something we've wondered about. You know, 007, most operatives don't last forty years in the field. Even those who survive every assignment generally retire before reaching that particular milestone. Usually there's some incident—a call a little too close, a rescue a bit too narrow—that prompts them to say, "That's it, then; time to pack it in." Sometimes it's just the obvious encroachment of age: the need for reading glasses to make out the hidden message, perhaps, or having to turn down a job because it conflicts with scheduled gall bladder surgery. You, it seems, don't have those little warnings. You don't appear to be susceptible to the normal ravages of time.

And that may be your most critical mistake of all. Your repeated rejuvenations and refusal to age beyond a certain point are quite amazing, and we really don't understand how you manage it, but in the end this may be your undoing. It's just odds. If you keep doing this *forever*, sooner or later your luck will run out.

If you were to age like a normal human being, then you'd be forced to retire, to live out your days in peace and honor, instead of continuing to risk your neck for Queen and country. We wouldn't keep sending you out there to face man-eating sharks, orbital death rays, steel-toothed killers, and the like.

For that matter, with your record you could retire right now if you chose, ageless or not, and no one would think the less of you. That you choose not to demonstrates either remarkable patriotism, adrenaline addiction, or a death wish—or perhaps all three.

Perhaps you prefer to die in harness. If so, then just keep on as you are, letting everyone know who you are, blasting everything in sight, falling into bed with every attractive female you see, accepting every assignment. Even if you continue to somehow stave off old age indefinitely, sooner or later the odds will catch up with you.

It may be fun, 007, but it can't last forever.

Don't say we didn't warn you.

———————

LAWRENCE WATT-EVANS is the author of some three dozen novels and over a hundred short stories, mostly in the fields of fantasy, science fiction, and horror. He won the Hugo Award for Short Story in 1988 for "Why I Left Harry's All-Night Hamburgers," served as president of the Horror Writers Association from 1994 to 1996 and treasurer of SFWA from 2003 to 2004, and lives in Maryland. He has one kid in college and one teaching English in China, and shares his home with Chanel, the obligatory writer's cat.

Agent 007
Performance Review
(A Human Resources Initiative)

To: Agent 007—Commander Bond
From: MI6 Human Resources Department
Re: Performance Review and Analysis

Dear Commander Bond,

The recent restructuring of MI6 has resulted in a performance review of all active operatives. The Secret Service is keen to maintain and, where appropriate, increase standards of performance across all qualitative and quantitative indicator ranges. As one of our most senior operatives, your work provides less experienced agents with standards to aspire to; therefore, your performance ratings are of the utmost importance for the 00 section. Your ratings have been compiled according to mission debriefing reports, interviews with key stakeholders, log books, records, and anecdotal evidence obtained during all mission phases. These ratings are tabulated below, where your personal ratings are depicted against averages for all 00 agents within this performance review period.

As noted in the table on page 126, while you score above the average on many performance indicators, most notably "Death Machines Disabled" and "Evil Masterminds Foiled," you score distressingly below the average on "Femmes Fatales Evaded" and, to a lesser extent, "Appropri-

Performance Statistics: Agent 007

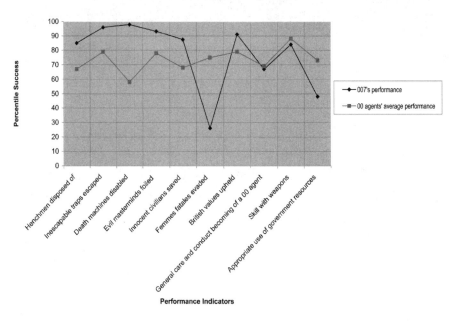

Performance Indicators

ate Use of Government Resources." The issue of your "creative" approach to government-owned resources has been referred to the budgetary oversight committee; currently, further evidence is being sought, and you will be advised of any action to be taken against you within three months of the date of this letter. In the meantime, it has been decided that the Human Resources department should address the other performance indicator scoring significantly below average—namely, your inability to avoid, foil, or evade femmes fatales. Human Resources is always keen to facilitate the professional development of all staff, and we have compiled an individually tailored report (included as part of this letter) and associated training course to help you improve on this identified area of weakness. This training course will begin on Monday at 9 A.M. and will run for three weeks. Upon successful completion of the training course, you will be allowed to resume your duties as a secret agent; until that time, new budgetary policies dictate a reduction of your salary by 45%. We urge you to look at this training course as a positive opportunity to develop your skills rather than as a negative outcome.

What follows as part of this letter is an analysis of your dealings with femmes fatales across key missions, together with specific incidents and areas of concern, conclusions, and recommendations in line with current departmental policy. We urge you to read carefully through the report and analysis, cross-referencing policy notations to the department's official Manual of Policies and Procedures (MOPP), a copy of which, in its thirty-four volumes, will be wheeled to your office today. To facilitate your knowledge acquisition process, the Human Resources staff has helpfully color-coded important aspects of the MOPP, and the legend for this coding is included in its own volume, as Appendix CCXLVIII. Please do not hesitate to call our MOPP helpline if you need further clarification on any of the policy issues raised. At the Human Resources department, our motto is, "Here to help!"[1]

Introductory Findings

Following the coding of the results above, the Human Resources department undertook to investigate possible causes for the performance anomaly in the indicator of "Femmes fatales evaded." After careful data analysis across multimodal domains, your failure to achieve a satisfactory result on this performance indicator has been attributed to three possible causes: firstly, an inability to identify femmes fatales on sight; secondly, suboptimal strategic evasion practices; and thirdly, overconfidence in ad hoc intimate liaison skills.

Identifying the Femme Fatale

The Manual of Policies and Procedures notes that one of the most important success factors for negating oppositional agents is early detection, and luckily for MI6 agents, femmes fatales usually share a range of common characteristics: foreign accents, dark or red hair, sexual aggression, and proficiency with weapons. In short, the MOPP states that agents are to be wary of any non-Aryan woman without a British or American accent, especially those who are evidently not helpless, passive creatures willing to do their duty for Queen (or President) and country. Indeed, the MOPP expressly stipulates that non-Anglo-Celtic women cannot be trusted: the foreign genotypes simply do not contain the moral fiber of British and American women, which is why foreign women are often easily manipulated by crime syndicates. The same genotypes are evidently responsible

---

[1] Please note that the term "help" is limited to the regulatory 6 assistance outcomes as defined in chapter 148, paragraph 6d of the MOPP, and should not be taken as a guarantee of unlimited assistance. Any assistance able to be rendered is subject to review and change without notice. Furthermore, the term "here" is relevant only in the abstract: the Human Resources department cannot guarantee physical co-presence at any location, and departmental functions will be outsourced to India as of the 1st of next month.

for female sexual psychoses, specifically the obviously unnatural feminine predilection for sex.

As one of the department's most experienced agents, it is incumbent upon you to adhere to the MOPP and set a good example, but on too many occasions, you have failed to take heed of even these obvious signs of femmes fatales, apparently ignoring their oppositional status and even seeking closer physical connections. Roundtable discussions within the Human Resources department proposed three possible reasons for this problem. Firstly, it was suggested that you may be unfamiliar with the contents of the MOPP; however, all agents are required to have a copy of the latest updated MOPP, and records show that the MOPP has been delivered to your office on four occasions. Interestingly, three of the copies were issued as replacements for earlier copies falling victim to mysterious industrial accidents; nevertheless, it was determined that you had had time to gain familiarity with all aspects of the MOPP. Secondly, it was suggested that perhaps your memory of the MOPP was faulty; however, rigorous testing of your memory in recent physical exams revealed an excellent recall on general tasks, and a superhuman recall on certain specific areas, such as the ordering of a deck of cards in a poker game and the tasting notes for premium French champagne vintages. Thirdly, there was speculation that perhaps your eyesight and recognition skills were failing, but again, your physical examination nurse confirms excellent vision, particularly at short distances, with an especial forte in recognizing rounded shapes.

Evading the Femme Fatale

Given that all tests suggest you should be exceptionally suited to identifying femmes fatales, it was determined that the actual problem may lie in your avoidance and evasion abilities. The MOPP states in chapter 377, section 4 that femmes fatales, like all oppositional agents, must be avoided unless absolutely necessary, and even then fraternization should be held to the minimum required to achieve mission objectives. Often though, you seem to have actively sought out these women and initiated various forms of physical contact with them—as often as possible—and in direct contravention of the MOPP. One example of this is your contact with Bonita, the belly dancer from the El Scorpio Café who was an agent for the Ramirez heroin syndicate. It is practically inconceivable that you were unaware of her allegiances, given that she had an exotic occupation, a revealing mode of dress, a Latino name, and a dark countenance, yet anecdotal evidence suggests you enjoyed intimate relations with this agent both before and after the destruction of the plant. This was both inefficient and dangerous, and resulted in serious injuries when you clashed with the truncheon-wielding thug concealed in her room.

A more serious case involved the SPECTRE agent Fiona Volpe. Again, this agent demonstrated all the signs of being a femme fatale, with her red hair, Italian accent, sharpshooting skills, and lust for speed, not to mention her SPECTRE octopus ring, yet against all departmental regulations, you actively sought her out for a more intimate liaison. Surveillance of the hotel at the time, together with subsequent medical records, reveal that during this incident Volpe made numerous dental incursions upon your person, many of which turned septic. You later claimed that the liaison with Volpe gave you no pleasure, although surveillance records suggest otherwise. However, even more seriously, you alleged that you performed "for King and country." The Human Resources department would like to emphasize strenuously that neither king nor country benefited from your actions in the hotel room that night and the total cost to the state for treating your septicemia was £312.75. Please desist from attempting to serve your king and country in this manner again.

As you are no doubt aware, chapter 38 of the MOPP outlines a number of approved evasion strategies for field operatives finding themselves in difficult situations. We direct your attention to section 14 of this chapter, which deals specifically with practices to use when faced with female oppositional agents. These strategies have the full approval of the legal department and have been checked for discriminatory language, cultural exclusivity, and suspect ideological positionings. Moreover, these strategies are useful in a wide variety of situations. For example, should you find a woman in your hotel room (a situation that seems to happen to you more than to any other 00 agent), the MOPP states that you should deflect the femme fatale's intimate attention rather than encouraging it, perhaps using a MOPP-approved statement such as:

"Your unexpected arrival in my hotel room certainly registers a positive physical response, yet may I suggest we initiate our interaction with a discussion of our respective life plans and key emotional expectations?"

As you can see, an evasion strategy should increase physical distance between yourself and a femme fatale, while remaining at all times both politically correct and constructively life-affirming. A similar strategy could have easily been applied to your encounter with Xenia Onatopp. While your actions in this case inflamed the situation, a MOPP-approved deflection might have extricated you from the encounter more effectively. Try the following statement for a valid alternative:

"I respect and appreciate your dedication to maintaining gluteal and quadricipital fitness, and support your rejection of outdated, stereotypical associations of femininity with passivity and physical weakness, but I would like to explore our social interactions from a somewhat less physical vantage point."

It is true that occasionally, intimate contact with these femmes fatales has resulted in positive mission-related outcomes, wherein the women have appeared to be persuaded by your "manly charms" to change their allegiances. This surprising discovery prompted immediate lab testing into reasons for this anomalous behavior and findings confirm the presence of pheromone B663 as an active agent in skin and clothing samples taken from you in your last physical examination. In the test samples, this pheromone was present in extreme quantities previously unseen in humans; the only animal known to exude similar quantities of pheromone is the rutting *Capra aegagrus* (wild goat). The Q Branch has managed to synthesize the active compounds present in your samples and aims to develop a new range of bioweapons; however, development has been slightly delayed, as Q was unwittingly splashed with a concentrated form of the compound and has since been given indefinite leave to allow him to rest and recuperate.

It can thus be confirmed that B663 is capable of affecting a femme fatale (or indeed, any type of female) when administered in close physical contact or even regular social contact; this explains the actions of oppositional agents like Pussy Galore, offsider to the nefarious Auric Goldfinger. Although your initial meeting with Agent Galore on Goldfinger's private jet must have alerted you to her femme fatale status, records indicate that you made no attempt to evade her. Luckily for you, while Agent Galore may have boasted that she was "immune" to your charm, it appears that she was no match for B663 when you eventually got close enough to "administer" it. But be warned, Commander Bond: B663 is not a foolproof safety mechanism and cannot substitute for adherence to tested and approved practices as outlined in the MOPP. Please remember that these affected women may return to their traditional allegiances once the necessary proximal contact is removed. In the case of Pussy Galore, a rational discussion of her evolving career path may have been just as effective as intimate contact, especially when phrased in MOPP-approved linguistic choices.

The actions of Helga Brandt, No. 11 at SPECTRE, highlight a related problem very effectively: your reliance on B663 and your overconfidence in your intimate liaison skills can blind you to the possibility that femmes fatales may counterfeit their response to you in order to get you at their mercy. Agent Brandt appeared to switch her allegiances during her interrogation of you, but the large drawer filled with sharp surgical instruments should have alerted you to the woman's sadistic streak. Although she gave you her weapon as a sign of her apparent unconditional surrender, you made inefficient use of it when you sliced her dress apart rather than using it to hold her hostage, and she soon had you at her mercy again, when she left you to die in a plane crash. Records note that upon initiating physical contact with Agent Brandt, you claimed that you were doing so "for England," but this was at best an unquantifiable and dubious quick-win; no bottom-line, actualized benefit to the state could be ascertained by the Human Resources department.

Furthermore, B663 may have a negative effect on some women, inflaming them to murderous passions. Such was undoubtedly the case with Fatima Blush. This femme fatale was already prone to psychoses, especially given her foreign genotype; contact with you disrupted her fragile equilibrium even further. Analysis of the mission debrief strongly indicates that your initial amorous encounter turned Blush from a normal oppositional agent to a crazed psychopath with an odd penchant for PVC pantaloons. Although only a mediocre henchperson, she suddenly became convinced of her status as a "superior woman" and demanded some kind of written statement from you to that effect (we note that the actual contents of that note have never made it to official archives, although an anonymous eBay seller is currently demanding a quarter of a million pounds for what is rumored to be the original signed confession).

This negative effect is unfortunately not limited to female oppositional agents: other females—even within the Secret Service—have been adversely affected by B663. Nurses and physiotherapists required to engage in close physical contact with you seem particularly vulnerable, and the high turnover of such staff attached to the Secret Service has been yet another unwelcome strain on the MI6 budget. Many of these key support personnel, including Nurse Pat Fearing and Dr. Molly Warmflash, have had to receive counseling and extensive retraining to recover from the experience. The retraining program was deemed necessary after three earlier female support workers changed their allegiances to SPECTRE when their physical access to you was terminated. The budgetary oversight committee, concerned with these escalating costs, has authorized the implementation of Regulation 1264—namely, that you will henceforth be treated only by male support staff. We know that you will join the budgetary oversight committee in warmly welcoming this cost-saving opportunity.

Counterintelligence Operations

In the past six months, MI6 has uncovered information from SPECTRE and other major crime syndicates under investigation which seems to indicate that these syndicates are aware of your poor performance in identifying and evading femmes fatales and are moving to take advantage of the situation. Even now, female agents are being trained specifically for seduction: they are highly skilled in the adaptation of the intimate arts for murderous purposes, and are armed with a range of biological, chemical, and mechanical weapons. Indeed, SPECTRE has already isolated and studied your individual pheromone, and now routinely inoculates its female agents against this chemical. In addition, rumors suggest that several crime syndicates are working on a feminine counterpart to your pheromone, which can be individually tailored to a victim's genetic makeup. This chemical compound, when adjusted to your genetic structure, will take advantage of your well-established proclivities and, once applied to the female agent, will render you incapable of resistance while having no effect on other men.

The imminent development of this pheromone could be devastating, not only for your individual missions but for MI6 and the British government generally. Luckily, there has been little success with prototype compounds to date, often because of unfortunate side effects. One compound developed by SPECTRE, code named "Hotferit," caused a rapid escalation in the body temperature of the wearer, leading to hot flashes, skin steaming, and, in one extreme case, spontaneous combustion (production and testing of this compound was abandoned after Blofeld's cat caught fire in this disaster). Another compound, code named "Magdalene," causes thick hair to sprout rapidly all over the female body, especially the face, chest, and back. Intelligence has been unable to confirm whether the "Magdalene" program has been scrapped entirely, but given the recent disappearance of Agent 005 after what appeared to be an amorous encounter with a yeti in Uzbekistan, it is possible that field testing of this compound continues.

Recent Performance Developments

The femmes fatales of your last two cases (involving the King pipeline and the Graves orbital mirror system) proved to be even more difficult for you to identify or evade, although it is acknowledged that neither Elektra King nor Miranda Frost exhibited a significant number of typical femme fatale characteristics. Nevertheless, it is only reasonable to expect that after so many cases involving these sorts of females, your skills in detection and evasion should be somewhat more developed than they evidently are. In the case of Elektra King in particular, it seems that despite all your training, you fell for the "vulnerable and helpless female" ruse. MI6 reluctantly acknowledges that there may have been some minor flaws in the attitudes of certain departmental stakeholders to Elektra King, which possibly influenced your relations with her, but reminds you that a proper adherence to the MOPP would still have ensured against possible negative outcomes on your part.

Finally, as to the case involving Miranda Frost and Colonel Moon, the Human Resources department acknowledges receipt of your recent memos regarding alleged faulty hiring practices within the department. You suggest that Human Resources should have conducted a more thorough background check on Frost prior to her instatement within the Secret Service. Naturally, the Human Resources department is as committed to upholding standards within its own ranks as within MI6 generally, and we assure you that your memos are important to us and we are taking your concerns under consideration. You will be pleased to know that the Miranda Frost issue is the subject of a current internal investigation but, due to legal constraints, the Human Resources department is not authorized to comment on any preliminary findings.

At the same time, the department notes that your actions with Frost were not above reproach. Surveillance indicates that you thrust your advances upon Agent Frost, subjecting her to verbal, and later physical, forms of sexual harassment in your attempts to engage her in intimate relations. Apparently, you not only suggestively demanded the "pleasure of her company," you also forced her to engage in some semi-intimate acts under the flimsy pretence of evading enemy detection. Given this evidence, it is perhaps fortuitous for you that Frost was revealed to be a double agent; had she been a model member of MI6, it is likely you would now be facing a criminal hearing. Under the circumstances, however, the Human Resources department is willing to suggest a mutually agreeable compromise: should the memos from your office to certain influential members of the MI6 hierarchy regarding the internal hiring practices of the Human Resources department cease, this department might be willing to overlook your unorthodox approach to intergender socialization on this occasion.

Concluding Remarks

We hope that this report has proved to be a helpful guide, assisting you in understanding your strengths and weaknesses in a positive and constructive manner. We look forward to your participation in the upcoming femme fatale evasion training course, where you will learn new, socially appropriate and politically correct strategies for your official dealings with members of the opposite sex. Please note that due to the discovery of your pheromone B663, no actual females will be involved in your training course.

Kind Regards,

Your Friendly Human Resources Crew

NATASHA GIARDINA lectures in children's literature and young adult literature at the Queensland University of Technology, Brisbane (Australia). She also specializes in youth and popular culture, communication theory, fantasy literature, and science fiction. She holds a Bachelor of Arts with first class honors and a Graduate Certificate of Education from James Cook University, and is currently completing a Doctorate of Philosophy in twentieth-century children's fantasy literature. In 2002, Natasha received the James Cook University Gluyas Prize for most outstanding postgraduate candidate in English literature.

So You Want to Be an Evil Genius

How to Avoid the Perennial Mistakes of Would-Be World Conquerors

I F ALL MY YEARS of watching Bond movies have taught me anything, it's how *not* to take over the world.

Sure, fellows like Dr. No, Goldfinger, and Blofeld have hatched some truly brilliant schemes (except for that weird bit about hypnotizing pretty girls into loving chickens, or whatever), and you certainly can't accuse them of not trying hard enough. But no matter how close they come to succeeding, it seems the same, predictable slip-ups doom them to failure every time.

Sometimes I think I could make good money offering seminars to would-be world conquerors, if only they were the sort to listen to advice. Sadly, their typical response to constructive criticism is to hurl someone into an acid bath. But let's suppose for a moment you're an aspiring evil genius yourself, and that you're willing to take an objective look at what things worked for your predecessors and where you might outdo them. What sort of lessons might be learned from what's gone before?

First, we know that to be a great Bond villain, you've got to think big. Common acts of evil like forgery, embezzlement, and telemarketing are fine for beginners, but Bond's foes are a more ambitious lot; they aim to break into Fort Knox, snatch space capsules from their orbits, unleash Omega viruses, and maneuver the superpowers into nuclear war. As Auric

Goldfinger put it, "Man has climbed Mt. Everest...gone to the bottom of the ocean. He has fired rockets to the Moon, split the atom, achieved miracles in every field of human endeavor...except crime!" Every great Bond villain believes the museum of human wickedness still lacks its one defining masterpiece, and he wants to be the one to paint it. Your first step toward joining the ranks of these van Goghs of villainy, then, is to devise a malevolent magnum opus of your own.

Of course, in order to do the job right, you'll need access to a vast personal fortune. Seriously, if you think skiing and golf are expensive hobbies, try taking over the world. All those orbiting death rays, submarines, nerve gases, and hydrofoils don't come cheap, you know. And that's not even counting the overhead costs associated with feeding your crocodiles and pythons, outfitting your troops in colorful jumpsuits, and keeping fuel in your fleet of helicopters. Naturally, as much of your inventory as possible should be emblazoned with a spiffy logo, so you can expect to pay big bucks for an evil graphic designer, too. And people being what they are, as soon as one of your henchmen gets a pair of poison-toed shoes or a razor-brimmed hat, everyone's going to want one.

Then there's the enormous expense of building (let alone heating and lighting) a high-tech headquarters under the sea, in space, or in a hollowed-out volcano. Granted, having a spiffy secret base is one of the coolest perks of being an evil genius, but take care you don't let it consume your entire operating budget. All too often, it starts with you thinking, "Maybe I'll put that old, empty supertanker to good use," and the next thing you know you've got a work environment so huge it takes a multi-million-dollar monorail system to get from the conference room to the cafeteria. At least decorating isn't a major expense; just stick with traditional stainless steel for everything. If you need to add a bit of visual interest here and there, consider some mood-enhancing designer accents, like maybe a shark tank or piranha pool.

The one thing you definitely do *not* want to do is install a self-destruct button. I understand the temptation; if things go awry, you want to be able to cover your tracks and leave no evidence behind. Let's face it, though; these things are just a bad idea. Besides the obvious risk of 007 finding the blasted gizmo and turning it against you, having a self-destruct button sends the wrong message to your loyal minions. It shows that somewhere in the back of your mind, you can actually imagine your schemes in ruins and yourself on the run. With that kind of defeatist attitude, you're never going to take over the world.

Once construction's begun on your evil lair, you'll need to assemble a

ASK DR. YES

Dear Dr. Yes,

I get such a pleasure from killing men. I like to crush them between my thighs, slowly crushing the life out of them, squeezing and squeezing as they beg for mercy, their pathetic feeble scratchings against my all-powerful thighs. . . . Sorry, I lost myself in the moment for a minute there.

Here's the thing: I think I might be a little too into it. At least that's what my boyfriend kept saying, until I crushed him to death. Now I'm crushing three or four men to death a day and my thighs are getting disproportionately developed relative to my arms. Can you suggest any exercises that can help me develop my arms as well? I'd hate to get out of balance.

The Georgian Flower

Dear Flower,

You might try crushing a man or two to death with your elbows once in a while. Variety, after all, is the key to maintaining a healthy and satisfying sex life.

In the meantime, my boss, Jeffery Mindow (1137 Sacramento Street, San Francisco, CA), can be a real jerk to work for, but deep down he is a nice guy, I'm quite sure. I think you'd really like him. I'd very much like to see you two kids get together. He could be the one!

No need to thank me.

Sincerely,
Dr. Yes

top-drawer team of second bananas, yes-men, and flunkies. Here we can learn some vital lessons from the mistakes of past Bond villains.

First and foremost, do not hire the hot chick. You know what I mean; every Bond villain surrounds himself with one or two hulking henchmen, a dozen to a hundred hired killers, and one lone female, invariably gorgeous and always the weak link in the chain.

Hey, I'm as human as the next guy; I understand the appeal of a pretty face, especially when your other employees are a pack of broken-nosed thugs. But the cold, hard truth is that it's just not worth jeopardizing your one shot at global domination to watch some cutie sashay around the fortress in a miniskirt.

You might tell yourself she has strategic value; she can seduce that womanizing 007 and lure him to his doom. Trust me, it never works. In *From Russia With Love*, SPECTRE recruits blonde bombshell Tatiana Romanova to seduce Bond and set him up for the kill; instead she falls for him and turns on her handlers. In *You Only Live Twice*, a helplessly bound Bond faces torture from SPECTRE's ravishing redhead Helga Brandt and her nasty collection of surgical instruments. She uses them only to cut Bond loose for a bout of lovemaking. In *Live and Let Die*, Kananga's inner circle consists of a fat killer, a hook-handed hoodlum, a possibly immortal zombie lord, and, of course, Solitaire, a sexy female fortune-teller. (Which of these things does not belong?) Naturally she's seduced by 007 and disaster follows. Most famously, Pussy Galore—a professional criminal on the verge of pulling off the biggest heist of her career—is completely reformed by one roll in the hay with James Bond and sells out her partner-in-crime Goldfinger, literally on the doorstep of Fort Knox.

To be fair, not every bad girl is swayed by a tryst with James Bond. Fiona in *Thunderball* and Elektra in *The World Is Not Enough* have their fun with the super-spy and remain happily on the side of evil. Until they're shot to death, that is. Fatima Blush of *Never Say Never Again* emerges from her dalliance with 007 as gleefully rotten as ever . . . until she explodes.

On the whole, however, hiring a female agent tends to open you up to more risks than you'll want to take on. And really, why bother if she'll be the only woman in the entire organization, anyway? Or were you planning to outfit the volcano fortress with a ladies' room and separate shower facilities just for her? When you're already guilty of nuclear blackmail, genocide, and missile toppling, the last thing you should care about is complaints from the Equal Employment Opportunity crowd. But if for some reason you feel you simply *must* hire a woman, then for pity's sake at least don't tempt fate with a name like "Pussy Galore."

While we're on the subject of personnel, one area Bond villains could really stand to work on is employee relations. In an average week, an evil genius will yell at his lackeys at least a dozen times and, if he's really cranky, kill one or two for good measure. Even on a good day, a bad guy's hirelings are transporting deadly tarantulas, operating atomic reactors dressed in "protective" suits made of plastic wrap, and acting as human shields for the boss when the authorities come crashing through the roof. Frankly, it's a wonder anyone still answers a classified ad for "Evil Underling."

Of course, diabolical masterminds make for difficult bosses in general, but the top men at SPECTRE really take the cake. Maybe when "Terrorism, Revenge, and Extortion" are part of the company name, maintaining a feel-good work environment is a bit much to ask, but this outfit seems to go out of its way to dump on its workers. In *Thunderball*, for example, a loyal henchman for SPECTRE's No. 2 man Emilio Largo bravely battles Bond and they both fall into a pool. Largo shows his gratitude by trapping friend and foe alike underwater and sending in the hungry sharks. In *On Her Majesty's Secret Service*, SPECTRE chief Ernst Stavro Blofeld starts an avalanche to crush 007, utterly unconcerned that in the process he's entombing several of his own troops. Far from being isolated incidents, these episodes are treated as a typical day at the office. Suffice it to say, the gift shop at SPECTRE headquarters probably did not sell a lot of "World's Greatest Boss" coffee mugs.

I submit you'll automatically be one step ahead of the evil geniuses who've gone before if only you treat your underlings with a bit more respect. Granted, flunkies can be exasperating at times, but try to remember they're as committed to evil as you are, and they only want to keep you happy. In what other field would you find someone willing to climb around on the outside of a moving plane just because you told them to? Cut them a little slack.

At the very least you should try to restrain yourself from killing your minions before Bond even gets a crack at them. There's nothing wrong with wanting to run a tight ship, but it's just possible that electrocuting your junior executives during staff meetings isn't the ideal way to boost company morale. The next time you're about to have a hapless lackey exterminated for reporting Bond's latest escape, stop and think about the effect on the rest of your workforce. Can you imagine the talk at the water cooler? "Hey, I haven't seen Schmidt in a while. Whatever happened to that guy?" "Oh, he gave the boss some bad news and got dropped out of the airship." That kind of medieval management style may remind the wage slaves who's boss, but it doesn't exactly foster *esprit de corps*.

Try to look at mistakes as teaching moments. An employee who's screwed up has a real incentive to try harder next time. Kill him and he won't learn anything. If you can't find it in yourself to show a little compassion (you are a villain, after all), then at least try some pragmatism. For every operative you rub out, you'll only have to recruit another one, and in today's high-tech labor market it's not easy finding applicants with an interest in good old-fashioned thuggery. It's not exactly a dream job, you know, living in a hidden fortress with no sunlight for months at a time (and only one woman!), not to mention wearing those goofy jumpsuits every day (the black ones aren't so bad, but some bosses insist on garish yellow or red...with berets, no less). Plus, word of mouth spreads pretty fast about a place like SPECTRE Island, where "training exercises" for new recruits include running past "teachers" trying to kill them with live ammo and flamethrowers. Good luck making *that* sound appealing in a recruitment brochure.

The problem with ruling by fear alone is that your workforce soon degenerates into a demoralized, surly lot who shuffle around your compound purposely avoiding eye contact with you or even each other. Soon there's no sense of community at all. Then one day James Bond waltzes in wearing a borrowed uniform and nobody even spots him as a new face.

Speaking of uniforms, my advice is to deliberately hand-pick a support staff for your hideout based on their body types. For all security-sensitive jobs, only choose personnel who are noticeably taller, shorter, or fatter than James Bond. Because if so much as a single employee in a hundred has 007's measurements, it's virtually guaranteed that employee will somehow end up in a position to get hit over the head and have his uniform stolen.

If Bond does manage to infiltrate your stronghold, there's a good chance he'll eventually fall into your clutches. When he does, try to resist the urge to reveal to him every critical detail of the operation you just spent years of your life and millions of your dollars putting together. I know it's hard not to gloat when a plan's going well, but blabbing all your strategies and timetables to a captive 007 is an indulgence that will only come back to haunt you. Just remember this simple rule of thumb: if you ever catch yourself starting a sentence with a phrase like "There's no harm in telling you, since you'll never live to interfere"...simply close your mouth and walk away.

Better yet, take advantage of the opportunity to kill Bond while you can, and I don't mean with an elaborate deathtrap, either. It's familiar advice, but no one ever seems to learn; it's amazing how many evildoers waste their one shot at 007 by overthinking the means of his death. For example, in *Moonraker* a gun-toting adversary catches Bond off guard on a private jet. The villain's cunning plan is to fire bullets into the plane's controls, then parachute to safety leaving 007 to plunge earthward in the crippled aircraft. Why he doesn't just use the gun to shoot Bond dead is anyone's guess.

Even the best villains trip up on this point. With Bond at his mercy, Goldfinger tries to bisect him with an industrial laser. Hugo Drax tries to incinerate him with rocket exhaust. Aris Kristatos drags him behind a boat over jagged coral reefs. Any one of them could have ended Bond's interference in moments for the price of one bullet, but instead they opt for needlessly complicated and thus escapable deathtraps. Even Alec Trevelyan, whom you might expect to know better as a former 00 agent himself, passes up a chance to simply shoot the unconscious Bond in *GoldenEye*, instead leaving him tied up in a helicopter programmed to destroy itself with its own missiles.

My advice is to forget the fancy stuff. Just dispatch Bond quickly and with no frills at your first opportunity. At the very least, don't waste your best food and wine by sitting him down to a sumptuous feast before his execution. For some reason, when Bond villains, from Dr. No to Scaramanga to Kamal Khan, find 007 in their custody, their reaction is not, "At last I'm rid of you... *BANG!*" but rather, "Tomorrow I'll be rid of you, but tonight, let's enjoy this gourmet banquet." Come on, this is a guy whose stomach is pampered with expensive cuisine and fine spirits every day. If you really want to torture him, serve up beans and franks with a can of domestic beer.

Another simple tip that can yield big results: make sure your employees know what Bond looks like, so when he arrives with some phony name, they'll recognize him straightaway. Of course, when a guy presents himself as, say, a "marine biologist" driving a quarter-million-dollar sports car and wearing a five-thousand-dollar suit, you'd hope it would send up a red flag right away. But by simply circulating a few fliers bearing Bond's photo, you can take all the guesswork out of it. Just think—a few dollars spent at the local copy shop could save you millions in exploded fortresses. (Frankly, Bond-spotting should be one of the basic, primary elements of training for all new recruits. Make it one of the cardinal rules: Always lock the entrance to the secret hideout, no smoking near the stolen nukes, and if you see the guy in this photo, shoot him on sight.)

You might even want to hire some assassins with the specific, full-time assignment of killing Bond. If so, consider deploying them as Step One of your scheme, before you've done anything else to attract attention. The time to hit Bond is not when he's already on the case, with his defenses up and a hundred secret gadgets from Q Branch tucked away, but when he's relaxing in a casino or on a beach somewhere between assignments. Maybe you could slip some poison in his *foie gras*. He'll never see it coming.

If you're going to make killing Bond a priority, however, you really should put some serious thought into it. In *From Russia With Love*, SPEC-TRE's ingenuous training program for assassin Red Grant involves dressing some poor guy in a rubber James Bond mask and telling Grant, "go get him." In terms of practical skill-building, this exercise is one step up from throwing darts at Bond's photograph. Still, even a weak plan is better than none at all. Three films later, poor old Blofeld's reduced to simply screaming "Kill Bond...*now!*" in an apoplectic rage.

This brings up another important rule: Never lose your head. A lot of common super-villain mistakes can be avoided by simply taking a deep breath and not pushing the panic button. In *You Only Live Twice*, for example, Bond flies his miniature helicopter over the Japanese volcano that very efficiently conceals SPECTRE's launch pad for a spacecraft. "Nothing here but volcanoes," he radios back to his colleagues, completely fooled. But then comes an attacking fleet of helicopters, and Bond figures there's something important in that volcano after all. This entire scene is more or less repeated in *GoldenEye* when Trevelyan shoots a missile at Bond's plane from a base that was until then perfectly disguised beneath a Cuban lake.

In both cases, things might have turned out differently for the villains if only they'd kept their cool. James Bond is far from the canniest sleuth around, but when you make the clues this big it doesn't take Sherlock Holmes to spot them.

Now, with all these guidelines drawn, you're ready to go out and make your mark as a super-villain. Before you do, however, make sure you establish a goal that at least makes sense. Cornering the world's gold market for yourself is a brilliant idea, for instance. Blackmailing NATO with hijacked nuclear weapons shows real moxie. However, trying to provoke the political superpowers into starting World War III may not be the greatest brainstorm you ever had.

Again in *You Only Live Twice*, Blofeld decides a nifty way to put SPECTRE on top is to trigger nuclear Armageddon. "When the United States and Russia have annihilated each other," he predicts, "we shall see a new power dominating the world." What's unclear is just how much of a world Blofeld thinks will be left to rule after a few hundred hydrogen bombs rain down on two continents. Similarly, in *Tomorrow Never Dies*, Elliot Carver figures news coverage of a war between China and the U.K. could earn his media outlets higher ratings, so he elects to start one himself. Since such a war would logically boost ratings for all the rival news outlets as well, it hardly seems worth the grief.

In *The Spy Who Loved Me*, Karl Stromberg at least understands the ramifications of a nuclear showdown. He *wants* the entire surface of the Earth destroyed. That way, he can create "a new and wonderful world beneath the sea." Even by Bond villain standards, rebooting creation would seem a tall order, but if global destruction is your cup of tea, it's vital to find employees who share your vision. Amazingly, Stromberg seems to have signed up at least a hundred like-minded, genocidal sea-lovers, but I wouldn't count on such good luck myself. Sooner or later one of your flunkies is bound to realize, "Wait a minute, all my *friends* live on the Earth!" Stromberg's also fortunate it never occurs to his troops that repopulating the planet—under the sea or anywhere else—will be slow going for a group comprised entirely of males.

My final advice to you, then, is to think your plans through. Find the evil scheme that works for you and have fun with it. Go out there and knock 'em dead...literally. These helpful tips, combined with your own high intellect and low cunning, will put you well on the way to global conquest. Follow them faithfully and you'll soon be on top of the world; ignore them and, like your predecessors, you may well find yourself hurled off the Golden Gate Bridge, sucked out an airplane window, or burst like an overinflated balloon.

Above all, be confident in your own genius and don't let that killjoy 007 rattle you. So long as you keep your cool, there's no reason you can't succeed. As Dr. No once said, "The successful criminal brain is always superior. It has to be."

Of course, James Bond dropped him into a nuclear reactor the next day, but it doesn't do to dwell on the negative, now does it?

DAVID MOREFIELD is a video producer and freelance writer with a BS in mass communications from Virginia Commonwealth University. Since 1996, he has served as an editor at *Mr. Kiss Kiss Bang Bang*, the award-winning James Bond tribute site (www.ianfleming.org), for which he has written numerous articles on 007 and his world. David's writings on Bond and pulp fiction have also appeared in the magazines *Razor* and *Thriller UK*. He lives with his wife and two sons in Richmond, Virginia, and is on the Web at www.davidmorefield.com.

"I knew Julius No. Julius No was a friend of mine. Osama, you are no Dr. No."

An Open Letter to bin Laden from Bond's Greatest Villains

Dear Mr. bin Laden,

We have been following your career with great interest, but you see, Mr. bin Laden, we are concerned that you will never become a world-class villain like ourselves. Face it, you wear a dress; you live in a cave and—we will try to put this delicately—you lack *savoir faire*. And your colorless henchmen are bringing you down. You are not Bond material but, as we see it, you have potential. We believe that, with our guidance, an upstart like yourself may someday hope to face a world-class nemesis like 007. We'd like to give you some friendly advice, one evildoer to another. Think of it as the Fab Five—Julius, Auric, Ernst, Emilio, and Kamal—giving you an "Evil Eye for the Bad Guy" makeover.

Lair. You have a real cave-design issue. A damp, dark cave filled with guano says worlds about your self-esteem, and we don't really want to go there—and neither does anyone else. You live with bats and blind salamanders. It's an embarrassment, but it doesn't have to be. Caves can be among the most exciting and dynamic lairs to hide from governments and their minions while putting your dastardly brilliant plan into place. They are meant to be remodeled with the latest high-tech trappings and should always create a sense of space and grandeur of scale. Think oversized lasers. Don't be afraid to accessorize; no cave is complete without a few hundred workers running around in sterile white garb or intimidating black jump-suits, doing your bidding—even if it's only busywork. And come on, those cheap rent districts of Tora Bora and Waziristan aren't going to impress anyone, let alone Bond. Think big—inside volcanoes, tropical islands, un-derwater caves. Like they say in real estate: *location, location, location.*

Personal grooming. In order to be a world-class villain, you need class. If you can find a mirror, take a good look at yourself. The crazed panhan-dler style might throw Bond off guard since he's accustomed to more re-fined social circles, but it does little to help your image in the international arena. Drop the white sissy dress and shave the rat's nest of a beard. The mujahedin beat the Soviets out of Afghanistan, you guys won—but that was over a quarter century ago. Time to move on. Quit trying to hold on to past glories. Move into the twenty-first century. If you want to take on someone as suave as Bond, you need to start dressing for success. Dump the pajamas for an Armani. Be daring—clip the claws, get a manicure, ped-icure, facial—go meterosexual. Make Bond want you.

Henchmen. You have a real problem when it comes to your support staff. What's with all the Number Threes in al Qaeda that seem to be caught by the Americans every other month? There's only one Red Grant, Odd-job, or Jaws, but the Number Threes in Qaeda seem to be as interchange-able as bowling pins and just about as memorable. Sure, you might not find someone who can kill with the toss of a hat and we understand you don't like working with females like our own beloved May Day or the very special Xenia Onatopp, but you need a henchman who is distinctive and memorable. Your henchmen are unremarkable never-beens. Your organi-zation is large and you should have the talent to promote from within, but it's impossible to recognize and cultivate a truly unique and gifted hench-man if you constantly have all potential candidates going on suicide mis-sions. Sure, it saves you on retirement plans, but high turnover rates can be equally costly to your organization. Invest in cultivating a henchman with enough pizzazz that everyone will recognize him. Think branding.

Mission and Message. You have a strategic planning problem. After 9/11 you had the world's attention, yet you squandered it with nonsen-sical ramblings, demanding that the Americans close their bases in Saudi Arabia. That's peanuts, and besides, your own Saudi government proved capable of kicking the "infidels" out on their own when they wanted to stay clear of the American invasion of Iraq. Since then you've been floun-dering, casting about for a real mission with a clear message. We've lis-tened to your tapes, watched your videos on al-Jazeera and, frankly, Mr. bin Laden, we can't make heads or tails out of them. We get that you hate the Americans, and that the rest of the West isn't far behind in your estimation, but your goals are muddled. You need something concrete—corner the world's gold market or control the global heroin market, maybe monopolize solar power. (You've already got the oil, so why not go alternative as well? Think Switchgrass—Bush already is.)

If an economic goal isn't for you, consider capturing the International Space Station. If Ernst could snatch both Soviet and American rockets, surely you could take over a single piece of aging, half-completed hardware. Saddam was imaginative enough to attempt to build one of the world's largest artillery guns, so it seems the least you could do is build a gigantic laser. Maybe you could take out the moon with it. Thanks to your longstanding ties to Pakistani intelligence, you have access to some of their greatest scientific minds to help you dream big. (Suggestion: No one has ever tried to create a giant water gun. Continents could be drenched while the oceans are drained dry.) If you want to be big, you have to think big. As they say, "The world is not enough."

Pets. Yes, pets. Affection for God's creatures can work wonders to soften your image if used properly. Believe it or not, Emilio's fascination with sharks really did bring out his warm and fuzzy side. Before the sharks, he was unbearable. And stroking the white Persian cat did wonders for Ernst, but we understand that you have a real problem with pussy, which brings us to your biggest obstacle to becoming a world-class villain: women.

Women. We've noticed you have a real issue with women. You spend your days and nights with only men. All of the photos and videos we ever see of you, you are with men. This has to change. So do your Neanderthal views of women. You see, Mr. bin Laden, the job of villain *extraordinaire* only appears to be about world domination, acquiring unfathomable riches, and power. It's not. The real struggle with Bond, James Bond—the epitome of polished, yet understated machismo—is about the women. The contest is about charisma, manliness, sexiness. It's about who will win over Honey Rider, Tatiana Romanova, Domino Derval, Holly Goodhead, Octopussy, May Day, and the other bombshells. So if you want to move into Bond's class, take our advice to heart. As long as you drape your women with tents for clothes and force them to walk silently ten paces behind you, you will *never* have Pussy Galore.

With darkest sincerity,

A collaboration of Bond's greatest villains

RAELYNN HILLHOUSE has slipped across closed borders, smuggled jewels, and been recruited as a spy by two of the world's most notorious intelligence services (they failed). The *St. Louis Post-Dispatch* wrote that "she's truly like James Bond and Indiana Jones all rolled into one." Her widely acclaimed first novel, *Rift Zone*, draws from her experiences. Her next novel, *Outsourced* (Forge, May 2007), is about an operative who becomes a target in the multibillion dollar War on Terror, and the only one he can trust is his ex-fiancée—who's been hired to kill him. A former professor and Fulbright fellow, Hillhouse lives in Hawaii.

Dress Like Bond

ANDREA CARLO CAPPI

WHEN THE MOVIE *GoldenEye* was filmed in 1995, Italian men's clothing firm Brioni conducted extensive research on James Bond's style, resulting not only in Pierce Brosnan's onscreen wardrobe but also in the book *Hero With Style*, a celebration of 007 not only as a gentleman secret agent, but also as a secret agent who dresses like a gentleman. It's true—though occasionally, in the '70s and '80s, the James Bond of the screen became a fashion victim of his age.

But let's have a look at how an elegant spy *should* dress.

A Night at the Casino
Since his very first adventure, *Casino Royale*, published in 1953, Bond has been portrayed as a gentleman in a tuxedo: in pocket book covers (white tuxedo), in the comics version by Ian Fleming and John McLusky (black tuxedo), and even in the 1954 U.S. television adaptation featuring actor Barry Nelson as CIA agent Jimmy Bond (white tuxedo). According to the legend, when Sean Connery won the role for the first Bond motion picture, the first thing director Terence Young did was buy him a tux and teach him how to wear it like a gentleman. The result is Bond's famous first appearance in the movie, playing at Le Cercle, London, in a black tuxedo.

A Night Out

James Bond does not spend all of his time in tuxedoes. According to Fleming, Bond's idea of dressing for a night out consists mostly of a heavy white silk shirt, dark blue trousers, dark blue socks, and well-polished black shoes (moccasins), plus a black knitted silk tie, with two white silk handkerchiefs in the pockets of his coat (as we see in the novel *Moonraker*, before the bridge game against Drax at the Blades).

A Night In

Bond might be slightly shocked when learning, in *Live and Let Die*, that Americans prefer to sleep naked, but he has apparently no problem with doing so in Istanbul in the novel *From Russia with Love*—especially when he finds Tatiana Romanova in his bedroom.

A Day at Work

Bond most often chooses a formal two-piece suit, usually left undescribed in the novels. In *Goldfinger*, leaving the office in an Aston Martin DBIII, he wears a yellowing white hound's-tooth suit. Shirts, possibly white, are of course perfectly pressed, thanks to that old Scottish lady, May, who takes care of Bond's home off King's Road.

Be careful with the knot of your tie. According to *From Russia with Love*, Bond does not trust a man with a Windsor knot, a sign of vanity and, often, vulgarity (this knot is typical of the SMERSH agent). Bond's ties are usually dark in color, although, when in the U.S. in the novel *Live and Let Die*, he wears a brightly colored one.

The movie Bond's most famous choices are probably the ones we see in *Goldfinger*; apart from the white tuxedo (worn under a black diving outfit in the teaser), there's the gray three-piece suit Sean Connery wears in the second half. (This suit was also adopted, along with the silver Aston Martin DB5, by Leonardo Di Caprio in Steven Spielberg's film *Catch Me if You Can*, when he was trying to present himself as a real gentleman.)

A Game of Golf

Before playing against Goldfinger, James Bond goes to the changing room. He changes his socks and replaces his moccasins with nailed Saxones and his jacket with a faded black windcheater. In the movie version of the golf match, Sean Connery wears a dark brown Slazenger sweater and a green hat.

In Summer

When not dressed for the office or a formal occasion, Bond's choice is a dark blue cotton shirt over light blue cotton slacks (as we see in the novels *From Russia with Love* and *Thunderball*). We can assume that Bond's look when in Jamaica must have been very similar to Fleming's at home in Goldeneye (near Oracabessa, or, in ancient Spanish, Goldenhead): a white cotton shirt over white swimming trunks.

On a Mission

Less common than a tie or a pair of moccasins, another fundamental component of Bond's outfit is the gun. In the early novels it's an Italian-made 6.35 mm "Beretta .25," which is extremely small, easy to conceal, and very precise. In the novel *Dr. No*, after receiving a letter from a reader named Boothroyd (after whom Fleming named Major Boothroyd, a.k.a. Q), Fleming replaced the Beretta with a German-made 7.65 mm Walther PPK. The movie Bond never had a chance to use the Beretta, since his weapon was chosen at the beginning of the first movie based on *Dr. No*. The Walther always appeared to be his weapon of choice (with the exception of a heavy Colt revolver he used in the final scenes of *Live and Let Die*), until the German factory launched the new Walther P99, which Bond adopted in *Tomorrow Never Dies* and has used ever since. But while it's easy to conceal a 6.35 or a 7.65 in a chamois holster under your jacket, the bigger P99 requires a Dal Fatto leather holster, along with another item we Bond fans are always ready—and extremely pleased—to use: suspension of disbelief.

JAMES BOND IN THE 21ST CENTURY

Why Do We Still Want to Be James Bond?

AS LONG AS I can remember, I've always wanted to be James Bond—ever since I saw *Dr. No* as a little boy. My mother didn't want me to be James Bond—not at that age, anyway. She wanted me to be a pianist. One of the first things I tried to play at the piano was—guess what—the "James Bond Theme." When I chose a different keyboard and became a writer and translator (of Bond novels, and others), I interrupted a long line of musicians in my family. I chose to translate Bond novels because, if I couldn't actually be James Bond, at least for Italian readers my name would be somehow associated with 007.

As a child I wanted to be a lot of things. I had a cowboy hat, a poncho, and a toy gun and pretended to be Clint Eastwood in Sergio Leone's movies. I loved Marvel Comics and I would have liked to be Captain America, too, though I never wore a red, white, and blue costume. I still see those movies and read those comics, but I no longer want to "be" those heroes. The trouble is...I never stopped wanting to be James Bond. Of course, it's more socially acceptable to walk around in a three-piece suit or tuxedo; people tend to notice if you go out with a "nameless stranger" outfit or a star-and-stripes shield. Still, that particular hero, James Bond, remains an icon for me. And, I guess, for many people around the world.

So, first of all…let's face question number one: Do we still want to be James Bond? I do, and I know a lot of other people who do, too. So the answer is undoubtedly yes, and I assume we can rapidly move to question number two: Who are *we*? Answering this, we'll be able to better understand why we started wanting and *still* want to be Bond.

Who Are We Who Want to Be Bond?

In 1963, according to Raymond Mortimer of the British *Sunday Times*, every man wanted to be Bond and every woman wanted to be in Bond's bed. Nowadays, I'm afraid, this assumption is no longer true for everybody.

I don't think the younger generations feel the urge to become Bond anymore. They might see the movies (luckily, otherwise EON would stop producing them); they might play successfully the video games (better than me—I just tried Electronic Arts's *From Russia with Love* and my Aston Martin crashed against the wall under Russian fire). But they probably don't read the books (though sales for the young Bond series might prove me wrong), and, most of all, they don't seem to see Bond as a role model anymore. Who might be capable of replacing Bond as a role model, I frankly do not know; it's hard to find a long-lasting hero in today's movies and literature, with the exception of Harry Potter, who has a different age target anyway.

Nevertheless, there are lots of people who still want to be James Bond, though these would-be Bonds are mostly over thirty.

My cousin, for instance. In the early '90s, at the age of seventeen—after I lent him my whole Bond movie collection from *Dr. No* to *Licence to Kill*—he asked his father to buy him a tuxedo. The syllogism was simple: Bond has a tuxedo; Bond has a lot of girls; *ergo* a tuxedo attracts lots of girls. His father's answer was no. Later, after seeing *Dances with Wolves*, my cousin decided he wanted to be Kevin Costner. After that he decided he wanted to become a Catholic priest (I don't know which movie led him into this; maybe *The Exorcist*? Or was it *The Thorn Birds*?) and he almost made it. The last I heard of him, he had quit the priesthood and was going to marry a former nun. I suspect a little bit of Bond remained with him after all.

Another example: my friend Edward, now over thirty-five, whose life changed because of Bond. It all started with a Corgi Aston Martin DB5 he owned as a child. When he discovered where that little toy car came from, a brave new world was suddenly opened to him. Now, not only does he wear the same three-piece suit as Sean Connery in *Goldfinger*, but he has turned the hotel he owns in Milan, Italy, into a museum of Bond memorabilia. Together we created the Italian Bond fan club, but while I mostly keep rereading the books and rewatching the movies, he goes on holidays in former Bond movie locations and spends his time trying to recreate the movies' stunt scenes, much to the amusement of astonished onlookers.

Another friend of mine owned the same Corgi car as a child, but he's absolutely not interested in Bond, hates wearing a tie (not to mention a tuxedo), and his favorite thrillers are the ones with realistic underworld anti-heroes, crooked cops, and decadent metropolitan settings.

I even know someone who *is* Bond: my fiancée's father, former officer in the Italian army who went on peace missions around the world and is a master in skiing and parachuting. He accepts no other movie Bond after Connery and is, much like Bond, the kind of guy you'd like to have on your side in case of a fight.

And then there are the writers. A friend of mine, around forty, who, apart from being a martial arts expert, writes horror, mystery, and spy stories, actually once bought a Saab 900 Turbo simply because Bond was driving it in John Gardner's novels, and made it the car of one of his serial characters. I know several other Italian spy story authors in their forties and fifties (yes, me too) who write series with their own characters, often very different from Bond, that still keep well in mind many of the lessons they learned from Bond books, movies, and characters. And sometimes those characters appear with a tuxedo and a girl (the two things still seem to be strictly connected—in fiction, at least).

Yes, we writers have our particular ways of "being Bond": something of what we found in Bond often comes back in our novels. My friend Jeffrey Deaver, successful author of *The Bone Collector* and many other thrillers, confessed once that his first short story, written as a child, was a Bond-inspired spy adventure (he refused to let me read it... afraid, maybe, that I might try to publish it as *The Bond Collector*). Now, occasionally, shades of the structure of the original Bond novels are recognizable in some of his novels, though they seem on the surface to have nothing in common with Bond. Think of his extremely creative use of the countdown situation—a use created by Ian Fleming in *Moonraker*.

Not to mention another friend, Raymond Benson, who turned from Bond fan into Bond author. He saw *Goldfinger* at nine and look what happened to him!

So I might say that *we* are, mostly, the boys who grew up with Bond between the '50s and the '80s. And so, let's go to question number three:

Why Did We Want to Be Bond?

That's easy. Take me, for instance. I saw my first Bond movies in 1970, when I was almost seven years old and my libido was just starting to say, "Hallo? I'm here!" I might have been precocious, even by Italian standards, but I couldn't resist Ursula Andress or Luciana Paluzzi. I suddenly understood what life was all about: fast cars, exotic places, beautiful girls....The opinion was reaffirmed when I started reading an Italian comics series called *Diabolik*, about a master thief with a self-appointed license to kill, a splendid blonde on his side, and a Jaguar E-type full of gadgets. (I have to say, with Italian pride, that Diabolik's Jaguar dates back to 1963, one year before Bond's specially equipped Aston Martin appeared on the screen.)

Later I rejected vintage cars as far too expensive and stuck to the girls. The Bond approach with women seemed to be effective: elegance, style, good taste in food and drinks; an ability to adapt yourself to any situation; cool, witty remarks in any circumstances, even the potentially dangerous ones; a ruthless smile...and, when speaking English, an acceptable imitation of Roger Moore's voice (it took me years to master Connery's *Shcottish* accent, but nobody does *that* better then Raymond Benson). The Bond style is probably what attracted even my fiancée a couple of years ago.

According to the movie trailers of the '60s, James Bond is a "gentleman secret agent." The "gentleman" reminds me a little of the definition of Maurice Leblanc's famous literary thief Arsène Lupin, *gentleman cambrioleur* (or "gentleman robber," which you might call an oxymoron: How can a robber be a gentleman?), suggesting that espionage too is not so gentleman-like. It certainly isn't in real life. During World War II, OSS master spy Allen W. Dulles used to play the role of the American gentleman at embassy parties (colleagues said the OSS acronym was for "Oh, So Social"), but his agents could not afford to be gentlemen in the battlefield. And eventual CIA director Dulles later may have become a Bond fan, and a friend of Fleming's, but there was no place for a gentleman in an operation such as the Bay of Pigs. After retirement, in a 1964 article in *Life* magazine, Dulles wrote that in real life there would have been a huge dossier on Bond at the Kremlin after his first mission and 007 would not have survived his second—so much for the "gentleman secret agent." Agents, like the aunts in P. G. Wodehouse's novels, "aren't gentlemen." And much of the appeal of the character is that Bond's job is to be an authorized killer, a socially accepted criminal who doesn't really like the dirty side of his job but still does it because of ethic and patriotic reasons. He is a ruthless assassin with elegant manners, a combination of good and evil in the same character. His approach to life is equally rough and refined, elegant and "manly": both sides appeal to women and provide a role model for men.

The truth is that, from a male point of view, Bond does everything a man would like to do: he drives the best cars, eats in the best restaurants, meets beautiful women, visits exotic places...and he doesn't need to be as rich as Bruce Wayne to do it. Most of the bills go to the British Secret Service. As a professionally skilled but otherwise unremarkable man, Bond embodies the average middle-class ambition to live a fancy life. Professor Umberto Eco pointed it out in a famous essay on Ian Fleming's novels (about twenty years before Sean Connery starred in the movie from Eco's novel, *The Name of the Rose*): Fleming spends more pages describing Bond's sensations while playing in a casino or driving a Bentley than he does describing action scenes. The reader identifies himself with Bond because he represents, if not familiar *experiences*, at least familiar *desires*.

What about a female point of view? According to Claudia Salvatori, one of the best contemporary Italian writers, the girls of her generation, who discovered 007 in the '60s, had a two-way identification with Bond: "That is, a woman," writes Claudia in the Italian 007 Admiral Club newsletter *Quarterdeck*, "can be both the male hero who gets all the girls *and* all the girls he gets, in a dizzy exchange of self-projections and identities that blows up every rule and reaches the climax in an amazing erotic showdown....Bond and the Bond women are not opposite, incompatible entities, but the same entity."

So, everybody wants to be James Bond, right?

Well...nobody really wants to be Bond *all* the time. Consider how many times he gets horribly tortured. Would you really want to be Bond when Le Chiffre starts playing with the carpet beater? It's true that Bond lives a fantastic life. But it's also true that he never knows whether his girlfriend of the moment will reveal herself to be a killer or turn up dead and painted in gold; he never knows if he'll spend the night in his luxurious hotel room or fall into the hands of a merciless villain, endure torture, and still have to save the free world.

Tough job, isn't it? But as Hemingway taught us in his books and Fleming summed it up in his *haiku* in the novel *You Only Live Twice*, your second life begins only when you've faced death. In a way, when good old James Bond faces death, he's reminding us not to waste any moment of our lives.

From Bond, I learned how to enjoy life with style. It's not necessary to do everything Bond does: I never tried skiing, or parachuting (this I think I never will!), or skin-diving. But who needs to, when you can live through

Bond with no danger attached? Instead, I try to speak as many languages as I can (only three and a half, at the moment), and I like to try local food and drinks whenever I'm in a new country. Of course, real life is different than fiction: last summer a doctor told me that I had to reduce my drinking and, yes, eliminate all free radicals (he then looked at my cruel grin and avoided suggesting I stop smoking).

And now, at last, to question number four.

Why Do We Still Want to Be Bond?

That's even easier to explain. We've spent all of our lives reading those books, watching those movies, and listening to that music. We still feel the old *frisson* whenever the "James Bond Theme" plays in the gunbarrel sequence in any new Bond movie. Our imaginations (or mine, at least) are still filled with Honeys and Pussys and girls fighting in gypsy camps.

But there's more to the picture that meets the (Golden)eye.

As Eco noticed in his essay, when Bond first appeared in the '50s, he was very different from the classic "little gray cells" detectives such as Sherlock Holmes and Hercule Poirot. But he was also quite different from Hammett's Sam Spade or Chandler's Philip Marlowe, the tough and cynical but somehow romantic hardboiled guys: Bond has something in common with them, but has a much stronger taste for life and lifestyle. 007's tragic experiences with girls like Vesper and Tracy anticipated some of Stan Lee's formula of the "superhero with super-problems" that now, after over forty years of comics, still seems to work so well on the screen. But in today's world, in literature or in the movies, there are almost no such heroes left. Contemporary movies might tell epic stories, but even the best heroes do not last long—probably because movies live short on the screen, soon to become DVDs and quickly disappear into oblivion. No one, at any rate, has been able to replace James Bond.

Moreover, nobody can replace Bond's style. In a world of global tourism, where visitors of foreign countries tend to look for the things they are familiar with at home, from satellite television programs to fast-food chains, there's no place for old-fashioned travellers like Bond . . . or Fleming: think about his book *Thrilling Cities*! In a world where appearance is more important than substance and people think that *expensive* means beautiful, Bond is the only testimonial left of true *inner* elegance. (That's why Terence Young not only provided Sean Connery with a tuxedo but also taught him *how* to wear a tuxedo.) In a world where, as George Orwell wrote, "ignorance is strength," a man like Bond, who carefully tries to learn everything

160

ASK DR. YES

Dear Dr. Yes,

My boss is a crone. She doesn't appreciate anything I do. My achievements—believe me—are practically superhuman. And I've saved her life, like, eighteen times. She says I'm a misogynist dinosaur. It's absurd. Me, a dinosaur!
Any tips on getting along with my boss?

Anonymous

Dear James,

Is that you? All is forgiven. That whole business with SPECTRE was really bad judgment on my part, I can see that now. I'm doing much better, and have almost completely regained the use of my legs. So I'd say we're even now, and no hard feelings. Come by sometime.

Your little Willie

he needs for a mission, from the tricks of bridge before facing Hugo Drax at Blades to Japanese traditions and rules when visiting Tokyo, represents an unusually open mind. In this television age, where so-called "reality" shows and talk shows give fifteen minutes' fame to people who should be ashamed of themselves, Bond is an out-of-this-world character with a lot to teach about style and elegance.

So we who wanted to be Bond years ago still want to be Bond (and maybe more so, now). He's the only role model left to us; we cling to him because he's the last testimonial of what we wanted, and perhaps tried, to be.

But this might be an intellectual vision of the character. There's also a more instinctive, less subtle explanation. Bond has been, since the '60s, more a movie phenomenon than a literary one, since the films reached a far bigger part of the world's population (about half, I'm told!). And Bond movies are usually fun, full of action and adventure featuring our favorite character. They bring us, or at least do their best to, the same emotions we felt as children. They remind us of the first time we discovered Bond's world and why we liked it. They take us back to the day that brave new world of adventure gave us a new perspective on life, something we don't want to give up just because life proved to be a little different than that world suggested.

Many of us started being would-be-Bonds when we were about seven years old. Well, maybe it's just that we simply refuse to grow up. We still want to be, forever, 007 years old.

———

ANDREA CARLO CAPPI, a thriller writer born in Milan, Italy, in 1964, created his own serial characters and turned into literary heroes two famous Italian comic book characters, Martin Mystery and Diabolik. He has published various essays, and a bestselling book on 007 written with Edward C. Dell'Orto. He has translated into Italian books from Spain, the U.K., and the U.S., among them works by Fleming, Hammett, Benson, Deaver, Kaminsky, Stark, Preston, and Child. With his publishing company, Alacrán, he's now the Italian publisher of the latest Bond sequels and Fleming's non-fiction, along with several American and European mystery novels.

You can reach Cappi at www.mondonoi.it/cappi.

Nobody Does It Better
Why James Bond
Still Reigns Supreme

ONE OF THE THINGS that made Clark Gable the undisputed King of Hollywood throughout the 1930s was the fact that he was equally idolized by his male and female fans. Men wanted to *be* him; women wanted to be *with* him. His masculinity, his confidence, his strength appealed both to men who desired to possess those qualities and women who desired to be possessed by men who possessed them. The no-nonsense toughness of rubber plantation overseer Dennis Carson (*Red Dust*), the wisecracking cockiness of reporter Peter Warne (*It Happened One Night*), the heroic, underdog brashness of Fletcher Christian (*Mutiny on the Bounty*), the charismatic naughtiness of Barbary Coast saloon keeper Blackie Norton (*San Francisco*), the noble impertinence and devil-may-care bravado of Rhett Butler (*Gone with the Wind*): through all these roles, Gable personified a kind of dangerous male who was unafraid of life—who was, in fact, larger than life. Of course, there were many other actors who were as masculine, as confident, as strong, others who could exude his brashness and cockiness; yet none of them had that "x" factor which made Gable stand out as the reigning monarch of the screen. He had all the same things that the other great male stars had; he just had more of them. If Clara Bow was the "It" girl, then Gable was the "It" man.

Alas, the Silver Screen has never been able to produce another actor quite like Clark Gable, but it has given to the world something similar in the form not of an actor, but of a character. Since his first appearance on film in *Dr. No* (1962), James Bond has thrilled male and female audiences alike with his unique blend of physical strength and verbal wit, earthy machismo and worldly sophistication, debonair charm and ruthless efficiency. He is a government man with a slight touch of the vigilante, a patriot with just the faintest streak of larceny in his soul; as much the international diplomat as the naughty schoolboy, Bond embodies Gable's ability to appeal to our love of the underdog while never losing his status as king. Whether played by Sean Connery, George Lazenby, Roger Moore, Timothy Dalton, or Pierce Brosnan, Agent 007 has continued for over three decades to embody, simultaneously, the ultimate Man's Man and the quintessential Lady's Man.

There is no doubt that Bond, like Gable before him, has "It," that he possesses to the full that elusive "x" factor which sets him apart from all the other spies and detectives and soldiers and cowboys who have graced the Silver Screen. "Nobody does it better," sings Carly Simon in rapturous ecstasy over the opening credits of *The Spy Who Loved Me*, and she is exactly right. But how exactly *does* he do it?

Accessorizing, Bond Style

Well, first of all, there are all of those wonderful gadgets. They may look to the untrained eye like regular everyday pens or watches, cigarette cases or briefcases, but they are really secret weapons, tools of the spy trade that allow our hero to extricate himself from any number of exceedingly tight spots. But, of course, the gadgets alone do not make the man. What sets the gadgetry of the Bond films apart is the subtle way in which Q's "toys" are used within the plot. The naysayers and cynics never tire of accusing Bond films of being overly fantastic and unbelievable, but the fact of the matter is, nearly all of the gadgets featured in Bond films are facsimiles of real gadgets that either existed already or could theoretically have been constructed.

No, it is not the gadgets themselves that are fantastic, but the fact that Bond always has exactly the *right* gadget when he needs it. How convenient, when the villain of *Thunderball* throws Bond into a covered, shark-infested pool, that he should have in his pocket a miniature oxygen tank with enough air to get him safely to the open end. How serendipitous, when in *Moonraker* he finds himself in another pool in the Brazilian jungle with a deadly python wrapped around him, that he should just happen to have in his possession a pen with a retractable, poison-tipped stiletto. And don't forget that exploding suitcase in *From Russia with Love* that (wouldn't you know) holds inside of it a set of gold sovereigns guaranteed to seduce the villainous Robert Shaw into opening it.

Interestingly, this narrative trick of equipping the hero with just the right device for just the right danger may be traced back to one of the first heroes of Western literature, a hero whose courage, resourcefulness, and sex appeal rival those of Bond: Odysseus. In Book IX of *The Odyssey*, the indomitable Odysseus is able to rescue his men from the cave of a man-eating Cyclops because he just happens to have brought with him the one thing he needs to defeat the monster: a flask of tasty wine with an alcoholic content that surpasses that of Jack Daniel's. Odysseus had no idea when he left his boat that he would actually need that particular flask of wine to save his life and those of his men, just as Bond had no idea he would specifically need his stiletto-pen when he got on the plane for Brazil. The fact that they have these unlikely weapons in their possession at the exact time they most need them does not so much stretch the credulity of the audience as enhance the mystique of the hero. These are no ordinary gadget-wielding adventurers, but creatures of fate watched over by some higher destiny. Fortune smiles on them and bestows them with the tools they will need to conquer evil and overcome the obstacles in their path.

Both the Greek sailor and the British agent are equipped to do battle in a dangerous world, but the screen spy has this advantage over the epic explorer: his high-tech toys are perfectly suited to his persona. For Bond's gadgets (including and especially his arsenal of fully loaded cars, jets, and motorbikes) are also *accessories* that the well-dressed gentleman simply cannot do without. The watch that doubles as a homing device or a power saw or a plastic explosive is also a fashionable timepiece that identifies Bond as a man of refined taste and sensibility. Bond, with the help of his gadgets, will always save the day, and, it must be understood, he will always look damn good while he's doing it.

Survival of the Wittiest

By placing so much focus on gadgets, I may seem to be suggesting a sort of hyper-Calvinist reading of James Bond, in which the hero is predestined to succeed and can therefore take no real credit for his triumphs. Nothing could be further from the truth. Despite his gadgets, Bond ultimately survives because he knows how to think on his feet and how to outsmart the bad guys. Indeed, though Bond is an expert in every form of hand-to-hand combat, he more often uses his brains than his brawn to defeat the villains and affect his escapes.

In his how-to manual for writing award-winning tragedies, the *Poetics*, Aristotle argues that the plot must never be resolved by a *deus ex machina*, some contrivance imposed from outside the play that rescues the characters within the play from a situation they can't resolve on their own. In many stories, novels, and films, the hero survives by just such a *deus ex machina*: unasked for and unexpected help arrives out of nowhere; the hero throws a desperate punch or fires a desperate shot and it saves him; the bad guy trips or blows himself up or has a change of heart. The Harry Potter films (and novels) are particularly rife with *deus ex machinas*—Harry is constantly being saved in the nick of time by outside forces that are generally unrelated to Harry's own actions and strategies. (*Monty Python and the Holy Grail* offers a classic parody of the *deus ex machina*: The protagonists are miraculously saved from a rampaging cartoon monster when the animator suffers a sudden heart attack and the monster promptly disappears from the screen.)

In a similar way, most movies that feature action heroes allow them to get out of any scrape by simply throwing a harder punch (Hulk-style) or mustering a sudden burst of super-human strength. Bond, on the other hand, honestly earns his triumphs, for they rarely happen either by a chance intervention or (excepting the over-the-top *Die Another Day*) through a display of unbelievable physical prowess. In the best and most characteristic Bond moments, 007 survives by doing some small action that anyone in the audience could do if he had the wit or the cunning to think of it. Thus in *Goldfinger*, Bond defeats the essentially invincible Oddjob not with his fists but by throwing Oddjob's steel-rimmed hat into a steel girder and then touching a live wire to the girder at the same moment Oddjob grabs the hat. In *Octopussy*, Bond twice saves himself from almost certain death by the simplest of actions. Bond is captured on an airfield and is being transported on the back of an open truck. Two armed men wearing parachutes sit facing him. Bond's lady friend drives alongside them in a car and uses her sex appeal to distract the two men for a split second. In that split second, Bond simply reaches forward and pulls the ripcords on their parachutes, whereupon they are instantly sucked out of the jeep. Later in the film, Bond is pinned to the wooden door of a shack by a knife-throwing villain. Seeing that Bond has been immobilized, the bad guy pulls out another knife and rushes at Bond. But 007 simply uses his fingers (which are still free) to pull up the latch on the door. The weight of his body swings

166

open the door just as the villain is about to stab him. The villain falls, giving Bond just enough time to free his arm and to kill the villain with the very knife he had used to pin Bond's arm. And don't forget the priceless moment (at the end of *Licence to Kill*) when Bond kills the villain (who has him at gunpoint) with a simple flick of a cigarette lighter.

No tricks here, no *deus ex machinas*, no impossible karate moves: just a witty and intelligent hero who is as spare and efficient with his moves as Hemingway is with his adjectives.

Fred Astaire with a Gun

And that leads us to a third aspect of the Bond character that puts him in his own unique category: his unbelievable smoothness and finesse. Though it may seem strange to compare a British spy with a license to kill to a singer and dancer with a flawless sense of rhythm, James Bond and Fred Astaire actually have quite a bit in common. Whatever these two screen icons do—whether it be on a pair of skis or on a dance floor, in the cockpit of a jet or in a gazebo in the rain, in the bowels of a submarine or on the ceiling of a room—they make it look not just easy but effortless. When Bond throws his hat, it *always* lands on the hook by Moneypenny's desk; when Astaire throws his cane in the air, it *always* comes down where he wants it to. There is a beauty, almost a poetry, to every one of their movements, and yet, despite the perfect grace of those movements, neither man ever sacrifices his masculinity or his unique sex appeal. Here, at least, are two men who have conquered the tyranny of gravity, of the stubborn, intractable resistance of matter. Even Gable himself could not inhabit a tux the way Fred did and James still does.

The lure of Bond is that of the suave, debonair man in the dinner jacket who is somehow essential for the preservation of civilization. We can rest easy at night because we know Bond is out there protecting us; yet, unlike the underpaid policemen and army grunts who actually perform this function, Bond is someone we can also imagine moving about in the highest ranks of society. What other action hero can match Bond's fine taste in clothes, in wine, in food, in women? He is at once connoisseur and gourmet, equally knowledgeable in art, in history, and in jewelry. He even plays a mean game of baccarat. No matter the exoticism of the locale (Istanbul, Japan, Egypt, Greece, India), Bond somehow fits in: always the cosmopolitan ambassador, never the wide-eyed tourist. He always knows what to wear, what to say, how to behave; he inhabits every culture even as he rises above them all. He is the true British gentlemen, at home in every society.

And then, of course, there are those wonderful, witty lines. He nonchalantly tells the megalomaniac Dr. No that the "asylums are full of men who think they are Napoleon ... or God"; he pauses, after flipping the thug from *You Only Live Twice* into a pool of piranhas, to say "Bon appetit"; when he steals a gold charm from the navel of a belly dancer (in *The Man with the Golden Gun*), and she cries out, "I've lost my charm," he eyes her up and down and says, curtly, "Not from where I'm standing." Just as he is never at a loss for the right gadget or the right strategy, so do words never fail him. Whether he is making a dry comment about a villain he has just disposed of or a sexy double entendre, he is always in absolute control. Indeed, as good as the lines are themselves, Bond's steely-eyed delivery is what really makes them work. Like a millionaire throwing gold coins from his Rolls Royce, Bond tosses off his verbal bonbons as though he possesses an inexhaustible supply. There is nothing stingy about James Bond.

Royalty on a Paycheck

And yet, despite Bond's overwhelming charisma and resourcefulness, we peons in the audience are able somehow to identify with him. Bond is not, after all, a totally free agent. He is a government employee answerable to a hierarchy of bureaucrats who are often quick to cut him down a few notches. Despite his lavish expense accounts, he is by no means an independently wealthy aristocrat. Indeed, for all his wit and charm, he is not an aristocrat at all. He is, in many ways, what Dr. No calls him in the very first Bond film: an underpaid British policeman. Especially in the early Connery films, Bond is often portrayed as something of an upstart who resists doing things by company rules. In *Goldfinger*, he literally has to talk himself out of engaging in a drag race with a pretty girl in a sports car. No matter how many times he saves mankind from the threat of world domination, he still has to put up with an occasional tongue-lashing from the choleric M, who won't even spare him a few minutes for sexual repartee with Miss Moneypenny.

Yes, the great James Bond has a boss, and, as such, he wins the hearts of everyone in the audience who must suffer under a similar tyranny. Though, by the end of the film, he has usually won the adulation of both M and the prime minister, he generally spends the first half as the proverbial prophet who is without honor in his own hometown. He is, that is to say, a sophisticated man of the world who is also, paradoxically, a hero of the masses. As such, he is like good King Harry who, in Shakespeare's *Henry V*, puts aside his royal robes one evening and walks in secret amongst his troops.

During the 1970s and '80s, when Roger Moore gave us his seven-film run as 007, the relationship between Bond and M tended to be a bit less sharp and abrasive, though Bond never fully lost his edge and was not above being misunderstood by those in power. More recently, the pendulum has swung back to the more disenchanted Bond of the Connery days. In *Licence to Kill*, Timothy Dalton spends most of the picture as a rogue agent pursuing a private vendetta. In the four Pierce Brosnan films that followed, Bond is given a new bureaucratic counterpart: a female M (played wonderfully by Judi Dench) who knows well how to cut her hotshot agent down to size. If Roger Moore's Bond has to learn to deal with the liberated woman, Brosnan's has to learn to deal with the woman in authority (and Dench, who has played both Queen Elizabeth I and Queen Victoria, knows well how to wield authority). If the working stiffs of the '60s could identify with Connery's rebellion against authority, the dispossessed men of the '90s could identify with Brosnan's struggles to assert his authority and male initiative over against M's threat of emasculation.

Needless to say, he succeeds.

Baptism by Sex

Which leads us to the fifth and final aspect of the James Bond character that has allowed him to continue his royal reign on the Silver Screen for over thirty years. Like Gable before him, Bond is the ultimate Lady's Man. Indeed, we read his masculinity as much in his physique as we do in the eyes of the ladies who gaze on him with such desire. Whereas the typical action hero is given one main girl as his companion and love interest, Bond is always given two, the first of which is generally killed by the villain while the second survives the film and ends up making love to James in a boat as the closing credits scroll down the screen. Bond's charm and charisma are overwhelming—almost a force of nature. He draws beautiful women to himself like the North Pole draws compass needles.

But Bond's sexual prowess alone is not responsible for his royal status. What sets him apart is the way in which his liaisons spark a profound change in the characters of the women he seduces. The fiercely suspicious and independent Honey Ryder (*Dr. No*), the frigid and passionless Pussy Galore (*Goldfinger*), the bitter Russian agent who vows to kill Bond at the end of *The Spy Who Loved Me*, the angry and domineering May Day in *A View to a Kill*: all are literally transformed by their romantic encounters with James Bond (just as Circe the proto-feminist witch is both feminized and domesticated by Odysseus in *Odyssey* X). If I may be allowed such an analogy, I can only compare this process to that of a baptism. Sex with 007 is more than just a pleasurable experience; it is a purifying one, as well.

In some ways, the prevalence of this almost mystical ritual is highlighted most strongly in those few Bond films where it does not happen. Thus, in *Thunderball*, the very naughty Fiona, who continues to work for the bad guys even after she has slept with Bond, taunts the British agent for thinking that any woman who sleeps with him will suddenly hear heavenly choirs and return to the side of right and virtue. (No surprise that she ends up dead by the end of the picture!) Indeed, Fiona is so shocking, so outrageous, in her refusal to be transformed by Bond's sexual baptism that she gets to do it all over again in *Never Say Never Again* (an unofficial Bond outing starring Connery that is actually a remake of *Thunderball*). Even better than Fiona is the lovely but wicked Elektra who, in *The World Is Not Enough*, not only proves immune to Bond's charms but uses her own sexual gifts to lure the male villain into serving her mad ambitions. (Elektra, no surprise, also ends up dead.) But the majority are not like Fiona or Elektra. For most of the Bond women, their romantic interlude with 007 releases them to be better or freer or braver than they were before.

As Peter Warne, Gable taught spoiled rich heiress Ellie Andrews how to be real, honest, and alive; as Blackie Norton, he taught the stuffy Mary Blake how to loosen up and enjoy life; as Rhett Butler, he taught the vain and egocentric Scarlett O'Hara how to step off her high horse and accept herself for who and what she is. Bond does the same, not only for the many women who love him, but for the men who look up to him as an embodiment of what they could be if they only had the courage and the class.

Nobody does it better? You bet your life.

LOUIS MARKOS (http://fc.hbu.edu/~lmarkos) is a professor in English at Houston Baptist University, where he also teaches courses on film. He is the author of *Lewis Agonistes: How C. S. Lewis Can Train Us to Wrestle with the Modern & Postmodern World* (Broadman & Holman) and *The Life and Writings of C. S. Lewis* (a lecture series produced by The Teaching Company).

ADAM ROBERTS

"An Englishman's Word Is His Bond"
Is Bond English?

L ET'S START WITH A list of the most famous individuals associated with certain nations. In some cases the "most famous person" is a fictional character; in some cases he or she is a real person, but either way they represent some essential quality of the nation concerned. Here we go:

- *Scotland*: Montgomery "Scotty" Scott, the Engineer in *Star Trek*. A Canadian.
- *America*: George Washington. An Englishman.[1]
- *Russia*: Stalin. A Georgian.
- *Australia*: Mad Max. An American.
- *Germany*: Hitler. An Austrian.
- *India*: Apu from the Simpsons. A scrap of transparent animation plastic "cell" painted with acrylics in Korea and voiced by an American.

---

[1] I know, I know. But look at the facts. Okay, he was born near the Potomac River, but both his parents were English (descended lineally from Edward III and William the Conqueror, in fact). Born in English territories of English parents makes you English, I'd say. Washington's youthful ambition was to achieve a commission in the British army, a dream he worked toward assiduously. He was a dedicated fan of the game of cricket, a game which separates out the civilized, English and Commonwealth on the one hand from the uncivilized and American on the other. Of course it's true that he ended up defeating the English in the War of Independence, kicking us out of North America, and governing as the first U.S. president—but, hey, nobody's perfect.

- *England*: James Bond. An Englishman. At last! Or—then again, perhaps not. Let's be honest: Think of James Bond and we think of a Scot first and foremost (you're picturing him now: the famous face, the Scottish burr, "Mish Moneypenny..."). Then there was an Australian. *Then* an Englishman, but nobody took him very seriously. Then an Irishman, who did a much better job. All these actors were playing a character created by a Jamaican resident of Scottish descent.

Something seems to be going wrong here. Let's take a step back. What about the other candidates for most famous Englishman, real or fictional? How about Saint George, England's patron saint? (He was a Turk.) King Arthur? (Most likely a Roman.) How about William the Conqueror? (A Frenchman.) J. R. R. Tolkien? (Born in South Africa.) Prince Charles? (He's prince of *Wales*, not England.)[2] Tony Blair? (Scottish.)

Okay: Are there any Englishmen *at all* in the building?

I'll hold up my hand. I'm English. I was born in Croydon, which is a palatial and utopian stretch of urban development to the south and the east of central London—I invite you to Google the name and check for yourself. I grew up in the southeast of England, and that's where I now live. I am thoroughly English. I'm polite to everybody, and especially polite to people I dislike. I watch football.[3] I drink alcohol. I am middle-class.

Let's not quibble. Of *course* James Bond is English. Who could possibly deny it? Fleming was clear about his fictional character's nationality. The next actor in line to play him, steel-eyed pobble-complexioned Daniel Craig, is English. And most importantly of all, James Bond embodies precisely those qualities that make an Englishman English. Look, I'll prove it to you.

James Bond as Englishman

Here's a second (and as it happens penultimate) list. This time it itinerizes what Bond's typical Englishness tells us about the characteristics of the typical Englishman:

1. He kills people for a living.
2. He has a great deal of sex with women.

---

[2] And to those of you who think that because Prince Charles is Prince of Wales that doesn't make him not English I would just like to say: I know it. It's just funnier this way.

[3] I mean real football. I mean that game where the players maneuver a ball with their feet. Not American Football or, as I like to think of it, American Foot-Hand-And-In-Fact-Whole-Bodyball.

3. He is extremely handsome and dresses extremely well.
4. He never loses his cool.
5. He's got a whole lot of gadgets. A *whole* lot. Man, he's practically *Captain* Gadget.

Let's take these one at a time.

1. He kills people for a living.

One thing Englishmen have proven themselves rather talented at over the last four hundred years is killing people. Start drawing up a list of nations with whom England has been at war at some point in our long history, and you'll quickly realize that it would be simpler to come up with a list of countries with whom we *haven't* been at war. (Such a list would include Antarctica, Munchkinland, and the geologically ancient continent of Pangaea). About a century ago a third of the globe was ruled by England. By "ruled" I mean that Englishmen had gone to these places and killed people until they'd agreed to become part of the British Empire. It's a striking thought: England is a tiny nation, without a great deal to recommend it in terms of raw materials or climate. How this place became the center of the largest empire the world has ever seen is something of a puzzle.

It is of course no coincidence that James Bond's adventures started appearing in the 1950s, and maintained their appeal over the second half of the troubled twentieth century. This was the period of the dismantlement of the British Empire, and the diminishment of Britain as an international power. This was good news, by and large, for the various peoples finally getting their freedom and independence after many decades of rule by a foreign power. But for many Englishmen it was bad news. Britain had been defined by its imperial identity for more than a century. The truth (that we are a small country on the edge of Europe) has been a bitter pill for many of us to swallow.

Therefore a series of compensatory fantasies began emerging: An English spy has adventures all over the globe, saving the world on many occasions. The great powers owe debts of gratitude to an Englishman.

The danger with these sorts of compensatory fantasies, particularly if they are prolonged over many years, is that they can overwrite the perception of the real situation. Because the enormous British Empire is a thing of the past. We no longer own such vast tracts of land. The English ruling classes no longer even "own" most of Britain, since legislative and legal devolution has passed most of the relevant powers over to Welsh, Scottish, and Northern Irish regional assemblies. The roar of Empire for the period of Bond novels, and much more so for the period of Bond films, has been a long, low, melancholy, withdrawing growl.

So, actually, "killing people for a living" is no longer what Englishmen do. Compared with Chicago or Los Angeles, for instance, the murder rate in London is tiny. We no longer possess an empire in which to strut around ending people's lives. Okay, I'll concede this point; Bond's assassin-chic does not reflect any present-day English reality. But there are still all those *other* things. . . .

2. He has a great deal of sex with women.

Perhaps you have come across the French phrase for a particular sexual practice: *la vice anglaise*. The English vice. Which vice is that? Well, since you ask, it was a vice of which Ian Fleming himself was rather fond. If you want me to be more specific, I'll have to refer you to a scene in the very first Bond novel, 1953's *Casino Royale*. Captured by the bad guys, Bond is tied naked to a wicker chair. A hole has been cut into the seat of this chair. You can imagine, without me needing to spell it out in graphic detail (I'm English, remember: our thing is *understatement* rather than graphic detail)— you can imagine which part of Bond's naked body pendulates through this hole. The bad-guys then thrash the pendant organs with a carpet beater. The word that occurs to me when I read this is: *ouch*.

Bond is being held against his will and tortured, of course, but if we imagine that he has actively sought out this experience then we have a pretty good working definition of *la vice anglaise*.

James Bond's sexual adventures may provide erotic fantasy material for unprepossessing and inexperienced young males, but it doesn't take a great deal of analysis to see this fictional promiscuity as a symptom of psychological malaise rather than a glorious celebration of sexuality. It takes an individual pretty repressed about sex (and for repression see number four below)—and indeed pretty tangled-up and revolted by the whole business—to take pleasure in being sexually *punished* to this extent.

The fact is that Bond hates women. He sleeps with women, yes, but he *despises* them. This is so thoroughly evident in Fleming's books that it makes them, I think, rather icky reading nowadays. It's true of a lesser extent of the films, especially more recently—thankfully our culture is no longer as tolerant of casual misogyny poorly disguised as "joking" as it used to be. But, in case this revision blurs our memory of the original character's attitudes, let's have a quick refresher course on one of the novels.

Let's stay with the novel *Casino Royale* (written in 1953) for a moment, since that's going to be the next film. In Fleming's novel Bond sleeps with a fellow British agent called Vesper Lynd (she later turns out to be a Russian double agent, and kills herself). He's unhappy that he has to work with a female agent in the first place ("women were for recreation," he complains). The sex? We're told that "the conquest of her body, because of the central privacy in her, would each time have the sweet tang of rape." When he learns of her death, he says only, "[T]he bitch is dead." Look again at those lines. You think this reflects an individual who *likes* women? (From *For Your Eyes Only*, 1960: "Don't be a silly bitch, this is man's work." From *The Spy Who Loved Me*, 1962: "All women love semi-rape." From *You Only Live Twice*, 1964: "This is man's work.")

How does this reflect on the English? Are Englishmen renowned the world over for their sexual promiscuity? Perhaps not. Do we all hate women? I hope not. I mean, I know *I* don't. My wife would kill me if she thought that.

3. He is extremely handsome and dresses extremely well.

Ah, the English. So suave! So well-dressed! So handsome!

Let's pull out of the air a list of certain famous Englishmen, excluding only the fictional ones (for their handsomeness, or otherwise, is entirely a matter of speculation). Behold, then, this list (and this is the last one, I promise) of gorgeously good-looking men:

- Winston Churchill
- Prince Charles
- Tony Blair
- Me

Now Churchill is handsome iff (which is to say "if and only if") your definition of handsome is "must look as though a freakishly large baby has been squeezed into a suit slightly too small for him." Corpulent, sulky, and with the look of something sculpted in the Jim Henson Creature Shop out of a half ton of part-melted wax: this was Churchill. He might have helped us win the Second World War, but *handsome*? No.

Prince Charles? A nose apparently stolen from the face of a much, *much* larger person, the bald patch of a Franciscan monk, the teeth of Donkey from *Shrek*. Handsome?

Come again?

Tony Blair. This is an easy one to test. Approach any heterosexual woman of your acquaintance and ask her whether she finds Tony Blair to be an attractive man. Her reaction can be measured by exactly how much she shudders in revulsion. This will be between "a moderate trembly shudder" and a "wild juddery shudder that shakes loose her hair."

And finally, me. Am I handsome? No, I am not handsome. I look, since you ask, like a cod with a hairdo. My mouth is like the TARDIS, bigger on the inside than the out, which means that my tongue and the inside of my lips are constantly trying to spill out into the real world. If my eyes were any wider apart they'd actually be floating an inch to the left and right of my skull. I'm not what you'd call a handsome man.

But this doesn't bother me. We English really don't do handsome. This is a country in which Elton John is a pop star. That's *pop star*—the idol who cavorts on stage in tight trousers to arouse screaming hordes of young people. Elton John. This is a country in which our most alluring sportsman is David Beckham—not bad looking, I concede, but a voice that even Pee Wee Herman would ridicule as too squeaky.

This, of course, is why filmmakers cast Celts or Antipodeans as Bond. There's nobody in the entire realm of England good looking enough really to pull the part off. So, in this respect, I'm not afraid to assert that the statement "James Bond is extremely handsome, and dresses extremely well" bears no relation to the reality of Englishness at all.

4. He never loses his cool.

Now we're really getting somewhere. Sangfroid, *that's* an English trait. No wild gesticulating, no raised voices.

But let's be precise here. "Keeping one's cool" for an Englishman actually means "repressing one's feelings." This is the heart and soul of being English: emotional repression.

Repression is now a word that has, for most people, wholly negative connotations. People will spend serious money to have specialist psychoanalysts banish their unhealthy repression. Except in England. Victorian culture saw "manly self-repression" as a necessary part of masculinity: Mediterranean types might gesticulate, and might enjoy passionate love affairs; the English never raised their arms above their shoulders, and conducted love affairs with stiffness mainly confined to their upper lips.

There's a part of me that delights in this, I'll confess. Maybe other nations have a more vibrant and colorful life, but there is something rather wonderful in never letting yourself get away from yourself. Something civilized in continuing to smile and nod in the face of tedium, annoyance, or idiocy. Tolkien once claimed that he spoke "the specialised politeness dialect of the Old Western Man"…that glorious mode of speech where the rudeness of other parties is met with a murmured "charmed, I'm sure" rather than a petulant rudeness of one's own. "I say, old chap, would you mind *awfully* not bashing me around the head with that cricket bat…?"

It's a wonderful thing. But it can't really be called "keeping one's cool." To keep one's cool one must have *cool* to begin with, and emotional repression is hardly cool. So if we are to insist upon James Bond as an individual who never loses his cool, we're not talking about an Englishman anymore.

5. He's got a whole lot of gadgets.

Ah, *now* we're talking. At last! A nation of gadgets. Thirty million men and boys in garden sheds or cellar rooms putting the finishing touches to their model railway sets. Amateur inventors creating bizarre machines. Wallace, from the Wallace and Grommit movies. *That's* English.

But wait a moment. Bond isn't the one in his shed (or the high-tech MI6 equivalent of a shed) making the gadgets. He's the person who coolly utilizes the gadgets, and then throws them wastefully away. The truly English person in this scenario is Q, not Bond.

In fact, Q trumps Bond on "trueborn Englishman" on almost every level. He's physically unprepossessing. He has no cool. He (I'm guessing here, but nevertheless) does *not* have sex with a string of gorgeous international supermodels.

There's only one conclusion to be drawn. If Bond is the quintessential Englishman, then Q is the true Bond.

How confusing is *that*?

National Icon?

The conclusion seems inescapable: Bond isn't English.

There's only one problem with this conclusion: of *course* Bond is English. He's the most famous Englishman in the world.

So what's going on?

Put it this way: Bond works not as gloss upon actual nationhood, but as a blatant piece of wish-fulfillment. Bond is not as we English are, but as we might wish to be. Of course that's not necessarily a good thing.

Most nationalities, I think, can argue that they have things about which they are proud and traits or associations of which they are a little ashamed. An American, for instance, can salute his or her flag with genuine pride— government of the people by the people for the people is one of the noblest and most inspiring concepts in human history, and the nation that invent- ed it and first put it into practice deserves to feel happy with itself. At the same time I daresay most Americans who put their mind to it feel pretty ashamed of bits of their national history—slavery, say, or the systematic eradication of a large proportion of the native American population. But for most Americans July 4th is a genuinely felt day of pride.

Nationality *can* be a strength; it can give a person a sense of belonging, an identity, a larger structure to their life. It can focus the positive aspects of pride, the urge to excel, even the impulse toward self-sacrifice. But we all know how bad it can go, when it goes bad. The rank fascist national- isms of the twentieth century—the wars and genocides practiced in the name of nationhood made those hundred years the bloodiest in the entire stretch of human history. We know where we stand on that. Pride in one's nation is one thing; racist nationalism is another.

My personal experience is European, and it seems to me that there are two nations in that ancient continent with particular problems articulating their nationhood. England is one. The other is Germany—a twenty-first- century nation of exemplary civilization and humanity that still, sixty years on, labors under the burden placed upon it by Hitler. But in one sense, judging by my various German friends, Germany knows where it stands. It was forged as a nation in the nineteenth century out of a long tradition of the highest and most noble *culture*: the very greatest European com- posers, philosophers, and poets were German (Bach, Mozart, Beethoven, Kant, Hegel, Schopenhauer, Heine, Goethe, Schiller). Although a hectic flush of Prussian militarism was present at the very birth of the nation, its roots were deeper, more civilized. For Germans today the Hitler period stands as a huge object lesson in how *not* to be nationalistic, a terrible and wrongheaded false step on the path of national development. Modern-day Germany has better things to which it can appeal when it talks about its self-identity—and when a modern-day German declares pride in their na- tion theirs can be a purer and better self-belief.

We English have not had this salutary lesson. The fact that we're still in- dulging in this adolescent compensatory fantasy of nationhood speaks elo- quently to the English process of refusing to acknowledge the hard lesson of our own history. Bond is a rather accurate icon of this: he is all about the hidden unsavory elements behind an apparently attractive exterior. (Sexy? Scratch him and reveal his misogyny. Cool? Repressed, more like.)

But there may be a way of reclaiming him. Let's agree to take Bond as a twenty-first-century *European*—as cool as a Frenchman, as sexy as an Italian, as expert with machines as a German...and as escapist and unreal a fantasy as an Englishman ever dreamed.

ADAM ROBERTS is a writer and a University of London professor, and he's English. He lives in England with his English wife and English child, just to the west of London. Actually, his mother's Welsh, but he certainly *sounds* English when you talk to him. Like 007 Bond, he is licensed. In his case he's licensed not so much to kill as to *drive* any motorized vehicle Category B (cars, including cars with a trailer weighing up to 750kgs). But it's still a license.

SARAH ZETTEL

Covalent Bonds

I LIKE JAMES BOND. EVERY time a new movie comes out, my inner adolescent smacks down my outer feminist, and we all buy a ticket, grab a tub of popcorn, and enjoy.

My first Bond was Roger Moore, and I fell in love on the spot (hey, I was young; we do that kind of thing when we're young). Later, I fell head over heels for Timothy Dalton. I eventually learned to appreciate the mature beauty of Sean Connery, and I was already in love with Pierce Brosnan from his *Remington Steele* days (I was *young*, remember?).

In those early, giddy days I thought I wanted to know everything about the object of my affection. So I went out and read some of the Ian Fleming novels.

This is when I found out there is not one Bond. There are two: James M. (Movie) Bond and James B. (Book) Bond. They might order their drinks the same way, but they are in no way the same character. They don't even inhabit the same planet. Book Bond lives in a hard, gray world of betrayal and personal angst. Movie Bond moves gracefully and freely in a world of shining wealth and beauty such as only Hollywood can provide. Book Bond, at least as written by Fleming, is mired in a swamp of outdated racism and misogyny. Movie Bond is a fluid creature, rearranged to fit the times and the audience polls.

Book Bond (leaving aside the racism and misogyny for other essayists) is a male fantasy figure. Movie Bond is a female fantasy figure.

No, really, explosions and all—and he's getting more so. This ultimate divergence of the two Bonds and the role they play is a function of media, time, mores, and the nature of fantasy itself.

But first, a word about the nature of internal, human fantasy.

Human beings fantasize. We all do it; we are always going to do it. We fantasize in private and in public, or with a selected confidant. It's not good or bad, healthy or unhealthy—it just is. Most of us know when to wake up and, as a result, our fantasy lives and our real lives amble along in a pleasant harmony. The mistake when fantasizing, or philosophizing about the nature of fantasy, is assuming there's no difference between what one fantasizes about, and what one actually wants and needs. Most men don't really want to be assassins. Most women don't really want to have sex with a virtual stranger, right now, just 'cause he says so. What we all do really want is a harmless and interesting emotional release that makes getting on with the day's business easier. When I talk about male and female fantasy, I'm talking about the fictional manifestation of world and character that allows for this emotional release, and that's it. I am most explicitly *not* talking about what any of us "really want." Okay?

Okay.

In order to provide the emotional release, which is one of the most important jobs of fiction, fiction must make a connection with the intended audience. There must be a sympathetic (you should forgive the term) bond forged. In modern, western society, men and women are, to an extent, raised in separate cultures. They are certainly raised, even now, with different cultural expectations. Whether the root of this difference is from nature or nurture I am not going to get into here. However, because the expectations the larger culture sets for our lives are different depending on our gender, it follows that the fantasies that are shaped by those lives and those expectations will be different. Men and women both have power fantasies. Both fantasize about sex, and success. But, in general, how those fantasies materialize is different.

Book Bond is not just Byronic in his brooding; Book Bond is full of self-loathing. He hates his job, hates the lack of honor and fair play in the world. He also hates the constant betrayal he faces, from the world around him and from his own emotions. For him, the only guiding darkness is duty. Duty trumps everything. Book Bond does what he does because he must do it. For Queen and country, he must. There is no one else. It's all on him. Everybody else is going to fail in one way or another, therefore he cannot fail or evil will be set free. In this, he is the literary stepson of Dashiell Hammet's Sam Spade or Continental Op. He must do evil in order to do good.

This kind of cold angst is peculiar to men's literature. Dashiell Hammet made a long living out of it. John Le Carre raised it to a modern art. Tom Clancy wrapped it up in red, white, and blue and tied it with a pretty bow. This taps into the emotional fantasy life of the modern male because they are the ones who are supposed to go out and support their family. To be an adult male in England, or America, is to work day in and day out to make a living, not because you want to, but because you must. To do otherwise is to fail at the expectations the culture puts on you. It is to remain forever a child.

Back in the Cold War, it was even more than that, and Book Bond cannot be talked about without talking about the Cold War. To be a dutiful, adult male of that generation was also to face an onslaught of change. It was a time of massive uncertainty on the world stage, even worse than the uncertainty we face today, post-9/11. In some ways, the Cold War was the obverse of the triumphant ending of World War II. This was a fight the world was making up as it went along, one that could literally wipe out that world, and it was being waged by a former ally who committed the greatest possible betrayal. It could not be waged in an honorable, stand-up fashion on the battlefield, but it still had to be waged and won, even though no one was sure how victory might be achieved or what victory would look like. So the angst of the character and his hollow feelings were not just personal, but tapped into the very real, very heavy political factors of the day.

Here Book Bond provided emotional comfort on a couple of levels. The cultural expectations heaped on the shoulders of Cold War men were not easy. They could be cruel and crushing and constricting. They could turn love into a burden to be carried, and they could make one, at times, profoundly lonesome. To have a figure of power such as James Bond facing disappointment and the cold reality of duty was a great release. It not only raised up the reader's personal emotions from the mundane to the operatic, it provided companionship in the face of the day-to-day struggle and confusion. Fictional characters, after all, are the invisible friends of adulthood. They understand what you're feeling and do not criticize you for it. Bond's depression and loneliness validated and allowed release of the depression and loneliness of men trying to do their best while their world was being overturned.

In addition, whatever unpleasant thing Book Bond has to do, he wins. His personal life, love, and honor might be a wreck, but he saves lives, potentially millions of them. In this, Bond was able to soothe feelings of uncertainty about the dirty little wars and the secret fights of the Cold War era, and these, at that point in history, were being waged primarily by men. To paraphrase a famous saying about fairy tales: Bond didn't just show that evil was out there. We knew that. He showed that evil could be overcome. Victory would validate all that needed to be done to achieve that victory. Victory would return honor to the fight, and in the end everything would be all right. If a man needed to suffer to do his duty, however small, to win that fight, it was an honorable thing. It was, after all, what men were supposed to do.

Movie Bond is an altogether different character. Right from the word go, the movies were far lighter fare than the books. Bond's emotional scars are tidily hidden under his tux. The over-the-top action and sex can be treated with a sly wink. Part of this is because of the nature of the medium. Film is, of necessity, a surface medium. Portraying the complexities of a character's interior life is hard in a film, and takes a lot of time and manipulation. Time is a precious commodity, even if you can convince someone that audiences will sit still for three hours and even if you're working from a short book. Recognizing this, Albert Broccoli took Movie Bond in another direction. He knew that what popular films trade in on is the visual splash, and that's been played up in the Bond films, unceasingly, with cool gadgets, explosions, cars, and even cars on the frozen lakes (has anybody counted how many times they've pulled that one? Seems like they've done it every other movie).

Movie Bond is all about the glam. He's a pretty thing. He's got panache. He may face betrayal and death, but he does it with style. And he doesn't hate the fact that he is constantly falling in love. This is an important factor when considering why he makes such an appealing fantasy figure for women. Movie Bond holds several fantasy elements in common with the ones offered by a sexy vampire or a tender-hearted monster. Here's this creature apart. It isn't bound by any of the normal rules of life and behavior. It's enormously powerful and has displayed that power all over the place, and yet You, as personified by the heroine, have power over him. He will risk life and limb for You. You can do what nothing else in the world can do. You can stop him.

That with Movie Bond there is really good sex involved in the fantasy is not beside the point. Part of the reason Movie Bond is a female fantasy and Book Bond isn't is that Movie Bond, in all his incarnations, is way, way, *way* better looking. And yes, looks do too matter, especially when there's not much else on offer. Book Bond feeds into a stereotypical and strictly male fantasy that a man can have every possible strike against him—he can be scarred and ugly, emotionally distant, guilt ridden, and hate the fact that he keeps falling in love (or at least lust)—and yet he can keep getting laid by amazingly beautiful women.

For women, you've at least got to have the looks, and Movie Bond has way more than looks. Movie Bond is tender. In addition to saving the heroine from the Forces of Evil, he gives gifts. He cooks. He dances. He takes time to seduce. He inhabits a beautiful, rich world. For those who think women are less visually stimulated than men, I point out that in the movies the clothes and jewelry are always on display and always gorgeous. They are as important as the cars and the gadgets.

The other thing about the glam in the movies is that they can get it right. Fleming very much wished he was a sophisticate, but unfortunately wasn't. He kept getting the details wrong, and not just on the martinis. Nobody in their right mind, for instance, orders room service at the hotel to get really good food, even in a really good hotel. Hollywood, which lives on excess and style, can correct these little details and give one a flat-out feast for the senses for which one never has to pay the bill.

The glamour that infuses Movie Bond's whole world is an important element for the female fantasy. The life of wife-and-mother, whether or not she has an outside job, is filled with dull, mundane, messy, trivial tasks. (I'm toilet training my four-year-old right now; *believe me*, I know what I'm talking about.) The ease, comfort, and beauty of wealth is a delightful fantasy for a couple of hours. In a Bond movie, you can participate in the luxury on ready display as easily as you can participate in the casual sex.

It is not commonly acknowledged that access to casual sex can be as much a fantasy for women as men. There is a desire for pleasurable sex that has no consequences no matter what your gender. Perhaps even more importantly, in the fantasy world of Movie Bond no heroine is going to be criticized for having or wanting sex. Let's face it, the sex lives of women, revolution or no, are still tightly proscribed by our culture. If you have sex and don't marry the guy, you're still labeled all manner of unpleasant things. At the very least, the stories tell you, you're going to be disappointed and bitter. You're still constantly reminded about pregnancy, disease, abuse, ostracization, sin, etc., etc. Even wanting sex is risky. If you're not beautiful, the media tend to treat your sexual desires as nothing less than comical in the extreme. If you're an old woman and want sex, you're a positive pervert.

But, in the darkened theater or at home with the DVD, the sexual fantasy is available. No one thinks the less of women for wanting James Bond and going after him. The consequences (if any) of sex with him are far different from the usual laundry list. In addition, after the sex, he's never going to make you settle down and stop being yourself for the sake of the children. A woman can walk out of this particular fantasy as freely as she entered into it, and that's a rarity for women. Movie Bond doesn't require a happily-ever-after ending. He doesn't commit? What a relief. For once, you don't have to, either. Occasionally, you can even give him more than he bargained for. I really love the scene in *A View to a Kill* when Bond gets into bed with May Day, and she flips him over onto his back and gives him what she's got. The stunned look on his face is priceless, and very much fare for female fantasy as well as male.

Lest you think the fantasy appreciation is limited by the gender of the character being portrayed, I'd submit that Movie Bond's freedom is another important element of what makes him a figure of female fantasy. It remains much more culturally acceptable for women to sympathize with male characters than for men to sympathize with female ones. Women, consequently, can readily share in the fantasy that is Movie Bond himself: the freedom of action, the wealth, the sophistication, the perfectly timed witty comeback. In the movies, women don't just get to have Bond—they get to *be* Bond just as much as the men do.

So why isn't this true for Book Bond? I submit it's because the attitudes against love and women are so much more blatant in the books. The manifestations of male duty for Book Bond are thoroughly removed from the manifestations of duty found even in the fantasy lives of most women. It's much harder to project your own interpretation and fantasy into the detailed interior life of the books than it is into the movies. The Bond movies, in case you hadn't noticed, always and famously end with him making love. Love, or at least sex, is triumphant. With the notable exception of *On Her Majesty's Secret Service*, Bond returns to the heroine, affectionately, humorously, happily. All wrongs righted, all hurts soothed, what Movie Bond really wants to cap off his victory is companionship and affection.

In the books, you get flat statements about how love is a weakness, grown women are constantly called girls, and sex becomes either a tool for manipulation or a grim act entered into only when the need cannot be resisted any longer. For Book Bond, love is never triumphant. Love is a weakness. The woman will betray. Either she will wittingly or unwittingly aid the enemy, or she will prove herself unequal to Bond's rough-and-tumble lifestyle by getting herself killed. Eternal duty, which is life to him, is death to her. All this combines to make it much more difficult for a woman to feel wanted and welcomed in the world of the books than she is in the bright, sophisticated, and ultimately happy world of the movies.

Of course, the movies have an advantage that the original Ian Fleming novels can never have: they're still evolving. Book Bond is frozen in time. The sexual revolution happened while Fleming was already in the depths of a long-running series (*Dr. No* was published in 1958; the women's movement didn't really pick up steam until the early '70s). Fleming, even if he had been interested in doing it, could not make his heroines evolve to fit with the rapidly changing notions of female strength, character, and sexuality. The movies could. In the movies, we could go from Pussy Galore, who needs to be shown why you need a man in your life rather than just a bunch of women, to Natalya (of the blessedly normal name) in *GoldenEye*, who rescues herself, at least initially, and works the computers in a useful and competent fashion to help save the world. Okay, the same movie gave us Xenia Onatopp, who drives me nuts, but we'll get to her in a minute. The point is, in the movies you can have Wai Lin, Jinx, and a female M. They are not only acceptable and imaginable—they are necessary. Movie makers need to attract a female audience. We've got money too, and this is not only a post–Cold War era, it's a post-Buffy era. Nobody expects the heroine to just stand around and scream anymore. It looks really stupid when she does. It is understood that if she is a truly worthy woman, she will kick some butt and take a few names on her own.

Which is another element to the female fantasy potential of Movie Bond. The female operatives are becoming independent agents. Jinx in *Die Another Day* is NSA. Wai Lin in *Tomorrow Never Dies* is a Chinese agent. Okay, they're not as good as Bond, but they don't get dragged into his adventures by accident. They jump in and are ready to fight the good fight right alongside him. They are companions, not just accessories or tools to get to the bad guy or the scientist father. Bond himself accepts them as such, although it may him take a little while.

This becomes another layer of the female fantasy. Without the heavily critical language of the Fleming novels, even the female villains have a touch of power fantasy about them. Okay, Onatopp has orgasms when she kills people (and what is *up* with that?), but she is also strong enough to take Movie Bond on in a stand-up fight. Pussy Galore, of the most famously unfortunate name, is a fighter pilot. Elektra King manages an international oil company. They may be bad guys, but they are not incompetent or passive. They are skilled. They are exceptional. Villains or not, they show it is possible for a woman to be more than a wife and mommy, and that she must be taken seriously. The hero ignores her abilities at his peril.

All media content is a product of its time. But it is also a product of the fantasy needs of its audience as well as its author. The books were intended for the men of Fleming's generation, men who were living in a rapidly changing world. The nature of work and war, those quintessentially male domains, were changing beyond recognition, and the change was causing confusion. The books displayed a moral certainty that could outlast the change. Duty always remained the same. There was always a job to be done, no matter how dirty or soul-altering. Duty matters, and it is the hero's job to fulfill it.

The movies fulfill a far different fantasy need. Rather than reassuring the male audience of the universal constancy and necessity of duty, they show the whole audience a world of freedom. Sex and violence have no lasting consequence. It's a beautiful, exciting, humorous race for 007 and whoever's strong enough to take the ride with him. Book Bond looks on grimly from the Cold War, while Movie Bond plunges headlong into the future, fighting Russians, corporations, terrorists, whatever villain we all need defeated.

Now Bond is back on the big screen. But Bond never left, and I don't think he ever will.

Pass the popcorn.

———

SARAH ZETTEL was born in Sacramento, California. Since then she has lived in ten cities, four states, two countries, and become an author of a dozen science fiction and fantasy books, a host of short stories and novellas, as well as a handful of essays about the pop culture in which she finds herself immersed. She lives in Michigan with husband Tim, son Alexander, and cat Buffy the Vermin Slayer. When not writing, she drinks tea, gardens, practices tai chi, and plays the fiddle, but not all at once.

James Bond:
Now More Than Ever

H E'S BEEN CALLED AN embarrassing relic of the Cold War who
should have been forcibly retired
and put out to stud a generation
ago, when the Berlin Wall fell. He's been called a fascist, a racist, a neoco-
lonial imperialist, and at the very least a shameless sexist, if not an outright misogynist. He's been the butt of jokes and the subject of parodies
almost from the day he first appeared in public, and he's been described as
a two-fisted, hard-drinking, chain-smoking, skirt-chasing, walking talking
catalog of every bad behavior that can possibly be exhibited by the human
male. It's even been said that all you really need to know about him can be
summed up in just two words: Pussy Galore.

With all of this embarrassing baggage, then, how can Commander
James Bond, C.M.G., R.N.V.R., possibly have a useful place in the twenty-
first century?

To answer this question, we must first ask another: who is he? Who is
Secret Agent 007, Mr. Shaken Not Stirred, Mr. Kiss Kiss Bang Bang? Who
is that man in the Saville Row suit, smiling with quiet confidence as he sits
behind the wheel of that silver Aston Martin DB5, caressing the grip of his
.32-caliber Walther PPK? Who *is* James Bond?

The answer to this question is not as easily found as it might seem. The peculiar challenge in assessing the proper place of James Bond in the modern world is in some respects quite similar to the challenge of picking the best brand of mineral water in the supermarket: there are so blasted many to choose from. Which one of them is the true, bona fide, and only Bond, James Bond?

As I often do with tough questions, I asked my wife. She said, "Sean Connery, no doubt about it. Very macho, very sexy, but with a roguish charm and a sardonic wit. Mm-*mmm*, Sean." As an afterthought, she added, "Just like you, dear." I decided to cut my losses and went to ask my friend John, the screenwriter.

"Definitely Roger Moore," John said. "Look, Bond is a joke. He's a superhero; a campy self-parody. He's the guy who can save the world without mussing his hair or spilling his martini, and Moore is the only one who got the joke and played him that way." I thanked John and left, and after that I asked more people, and got more answers. Some preferred Connery; others, Moore. Younger folks were more likely to pick Pierce Brosnan, and Timothy Dalton has his fans. No one would admit to liking George Lazenby.

But in the end, all my questioning proved fruitless. Everyone it seems has a favorite Bond, and not one single person answered, "James *who*?" All that my investigative efforts really produced was a wealth of opinions about the actors who had played the role, what they'd looked like while doing it, and how they'd played it. Along with a favorite Bond actor, it seems everyone has a favorite Bond villain, a favorite Bond girl, a favorite Bond car, a favorite Bond stunt, and a favorite Bond improbable gadget. None of these opinions helped me to get any closer to resolving the crucial issue of just who Bond is, though, and I still had no good answer to the question that lies at the heart of this essay: what is it about James Bond that saves him from occupying a prominent place in the dustbin of history, right next to Matt Helm?

So I went to the source.

The Gospel According to Ian

The portrait of Bond that emerges from Ian Fleming's original novels and short stories is markedly different from the collage that can be assembled by watching a series of twenty-some movies filmed over a span of forty-some years. For one thing, Fleming's Bond doesn't look much like any of the actors who have ever played him onscreen. In the words of Vesper Lynd in Fleming's first novel, *Casino Royale*: "He is very good looking. He reminds me rather of Hoagy Carmichael, but there is something cold and ruthless in his...." (Whatever Mademoiselle Lynd intended to say next, of course, was forever lost in the explosion that blew in the front windows of the Hermitage bar. These sorts of conversation-stoppers happen all the time around Mr. Bond.)

For another thing, it's important to note that the novels and movies were not made in the same chronological order. Bond's literary life begins with *Casino Royale* (1953), followed by *Live and Let Die* (1954), *Moonraker* (1955), *Diamonds Are Forever* (1956), *From Russia With Love* (1957), *Dr. No* (1958), and *Goldfinger* (1959). His cinematic life, on the other hand, began a decade later with *Dr. No* (1962), and continued with *From Russia With Love* (1963), *Goldfinger* (1964), and *Thunderball* (1965). In some cases this resequencing of his story merely introduces continuity problems: for example, *On Her Majesty's Secret Service* was written and set before *You Only Live Twice*, and at the end of the latter book arch-villain Ernst Stavro Blofeld is not merely dead, he is really most sincerely dead. But in the movies the sequence of these stories is reversed, so it became necessary for the moviemakers to equip Blofeld with the sort of cheesy last-ditch escape devices that Mike Myers later parodied to such great effect in *Austin Powers*. In still other cases—*Moonraker*, for example—it apparently proved more expedient to simply junk Fleming's original story completely and start over from scratch, the result being that many of the later movies, and in particular the movies from the Roger Moore era, bear naught but an in-name-only relationship to the eponymous novels. This is a very important point, and we'll return to it momentarily.

For a third thing, though, a reading of Fleming's original novels quickly leads to the realization that Bond's origins and backstory are in constant flux. In *Casino Royale*, for example, we get this small insight into Bond's private life: "Bond's car was his only personal hobby. One of the last of the 4-litre Bentleys with the supercharger by Amherst Villiers, he had bought it almost new in 1933 and had kept it in careful storage through the war." Two years later, in *Moonraker*, Bond is described as being only eight years away from mandatory retirement at age forty-five, and yet nine years after that, in *You Only Live Twice*, Bond's official obituary states that in 1941 he dropped out of school at age seventeen to enlist in the Royal Navy. From these apparent contradictions, and many more like them, we must draw one of only two possible conclusions: either Bond's parents in 1933 were far more indulgent with their nine-year-old son than all but the worst of modern American parents, or else even Fleming himself didn't give a rip about keeping Bond's backstory straight. And if we can't trust the putative facts put forth by his creator, then what hope do we have to know *anything* about the real James Bond?

What we can know is that which we are left with: his mood, tone, and character. In this regard, Fleming was quite consistent. Bond, as written by Fleming, was neither the wry stud-muffin played by Connery, the smirking quipster played by Moore, nor the smart-but-tough human action-figure played by Brosnan. Bond was a *film noir* character from the get-go, who had less in common with his later cinematic portrayals than with his literary contemporaries and immediate predecessors: Mike Hammer, Sam Spade, Simon Templar, and the Continental Op. Fleming's Bond was a *thug*. He could pass for a gentleman when required, but underneath the civilized veneer he was a cold-blooded killer in the employ of Her Majesty's government. He could slit a sleeping man's throat or kill someone with his bare hands and feel little more afterward than the need for a good stiff drink. He could make love to a woman in chapter five and shoot her in the back in chapter six. He was, as Fleming described him, "a neutral figure—an anonymous blunt instrument wielded by a Government Department." He was meant to be an emotionally detached and utterly deadly assassin, a man who got involved in interesting business but was not himself interesting. In short, Bond was—ironically—meant by Fleming to be most like the least-liked of his big-screen avatars: George Lazenby.

When you start hanging about with Bond, you'll note, it is difficult to avoid becoming drenched in irony.

Will the Real James Bond Please Stand Up?

With this larger realization, many smaller ones finally begin to fall into place. The first is that the real James Bond is not the literary one that Ian Fleming created; it's the ever-changing succession of movie Bonds who have appeared in the decades since. Without the movies James Bond would now be just another nearly forgotten fifty-year-old hard-boiled pulp thriller character, right up there with Sexton Blake or the Black Bat. Ian Fleming may have supplied the original template, but as with the tales of King Arthur or Charlemagne, it is the subsequent retelling and reshaping of these stories by others that has made Bond a legend.

The second realization is that there is no one true Bond. They are all true; even David Niven in the 1967 version of *Casino Royale*. Like all good legendary characters, Bond is profoundly malleable and often allegorical. He is an ageless hero, with no reliably fixed beginning and no apparent end in sight. His movies function as mirrors to their respective times, and the

192

tales of Bond's many adventures most strongly reflect the worries, hopes, fears, and joys of those who are telling the tales, and those who are eagerly listening. When considering the question of whether the world still needs Bond, then, it's important not to let the then-contemporary trappings of previous tellings of his deeds interfere with the essential truths that he embodies.

But again, we'll come back to this one in a bit.

The third realization is that deep down, in his heart of hearts, the real James Bond is *not* a spy. Yes, he ostensibly is an employee of a real intelligence agency, MI6, and his adventures take place in countries with real names and cities you can find on a map. But disregarding for a moment the oxymoronic concept of a *famous* secret agent, any attempt to draw a correlation between Bond's gallivanting about the globe on a seemingly bottomless expense account and the tedious process of real covert intelligence work—

A Smart Slap in the Face with the Cold Wet Washcloth of Reality

Okay, look. We could do the whole Tom Clancy thing here, get bogged down in acronymspeak, and lard this discussion with terms like HUMINT, ELINT, and SIGINT. We could discuss the relative effectiveness of various KGB and Mossad "wet work" methods, debate the usefulness of the Mersenne Twister 19337 algorithm in cryptography, or wander off into a long and tedious explication of cut-outs, dead drops, false flag operations, and all the other baroque feints and shadows that are the tools of the trade in the espionage business. But before we go any further, there are a few essential concepts you simply must understand.

Intelligence is all about discovering what your potential enemy's plans and abilities are before he can use them against you. *Counterintelligence* is all about preventing your enemy from doing the same to you. Now, the perfect intelligence operation is one in which the enemy's secrets are learned without his ever suspecting that his secrets are no longer secret. The perfect counterintelligence operation is one in which the enemy's plans are disrupted before he can put them into effect and he blames only himself for their failure. *Never* should you let your enemy know just who exactly it is who has foiled his plans or how, because, like a parlor magic trick, an intelligence method that has been stripped of its veil of secrecy is an intelligence method that no longer works.

And yes, while even "nice" governments have from time to time used assassins as instruments of policy, no one in their right mind would ever employ a man such as Bond in this role, if only for fear that he might some-day retire from the service and publish his memoirs. Instead, the grisly truth is that assassins should be *disposable* people. The ideal assassin is an illiterate and mute suicide bomber: he can't talk if captured, there's little risk he'll abort the mission if he finds that his escape route is blocked, and if he succeeds there is absolutely no chance of his ever coming back later and demanding more money to stay silent. A passable second choice is a man such as Mehmet Ali Ağca, the attempted assassin of Pope John Paul II. While many believe this operation was run by the Bulgarian Secret Ser-vice acting as a cut-out for the KGB, and Ağca himself was captured and has talked at length, there is little chance of ever learning the truth from his testimony. Ağca has spun tales of enormous conspiracies-within-con-spiracies, and has at various times claimed to be a Bulgarian agent, a CIA agent, a Palestinian militant, an Italian military intelligence agent, an em-ployee of a dissident faction in the Vatican Bank, and the second coming of Jesus Christ, here to fulfill the Third Prophecy of Fatima.

As I've said before: When it comes to the world of espionage, the truth is as slippery as a salamander in a jar of Vaseline.

In any case, a well-executed intelligence, counterintelligence, or assas-sination operation *never* requires sending in a lone agent to perform feats of derring-do, effect hair's-breadth escapes, fight desperate battles against legions of hapless minions, completely demolish the enemy's citadel in a cataclysmic fiery blast, or end up in a rubber life-raft with a rescued beau-tiful maiden. Are we all clear on this?

Good, because here is a case in point. In April of 1943, U.S. naval intel-ligence codebreakers intercepted and decrypted radio messages giving the exact whereabouts and travel plans of Admiral Isoroku Yamamoto, Japan's supreme naval commander and the architect of the attack on Pearl Har-bor. Now, if Bond had even a tenuous rooting in reality, the British Secret Service's Special Operations Executive clearly would have responded to this information by sending in a lone undercover agent with an underpow-ered handgun. Posing as a Dutch East Indian rubber plantation owner, this British agent would no doubt have easily dispatched several dim-witted henchmen, had a quick but torrid roll on the futon with Yamamoto's per-sonal secretary and mistress, Kissy Suzuki, fought a thrilling *katana* duel with Yamamoto's master assassin, Oddjob, been captured and then rescued from certain death at the last moment by the beautiful French Polynesian girl Improbable Chance, and in the final nick of time completed his mis-sion by killing Yamamoto and narrowly escaping from the subsequent fiery explosion of Yamamoto's secret lair to end up floating in a rubber life-raft with Ms. Chance somewhere in the Java Sea.

As it happened, though, the Americans were in charge of this operation, so they instead sent in a squadron of P-38 fighters to blast the living day-lights out of Yamamoto's military transport, the decoy transport, his fighter escort, and anyone else who happened to be in the general vicinity at about the same time. Yet for the remainder of the war, the Japanese continued to believe that Yamamoto's flight plan had been discovered and betrayed by native coast-watchers, and failed to realize that the Americans had broken their naval codes and were reading their most secret communiques.

There. *This* is what a successful license-to-kill intelligence operation looks like in the real world.

So Who Is This Bond Fellow, Anyway?

If Bond has no place in the world of real espionage, and if the details of his life, his adventures, and even his face may be changed and changed again at the storyteller's discretion, then where does he belong? Once again, we're back to the challenge of trying to identify the one true Bond with only mood, tone, and character to work with, so let's consider the things about him that never change from one tale to the next.

Bond is a *warrior*. He never serves mere political expedience or con-venience. If any government actually had a man like Bond on the payroll they'd be unable resist the temptation to have him knock off a bothersome reporter or two every now and then, but Bond never does that. Instead, he fights only clearly identifiable villains who are at least his equals, if not more powerful. More to the point, he fights only enemies that *can* be de-feated. In Bond's world there are no insoluble problems or lingering diplo-matic ambiguities.

Bond has a *code of honor*. He may have a license to kill, but he does so only reluctantly and takes no pleasure in doing it. He will try the disabling knee or shoulder shot rather than the killing shot if he can. (Except when battling his way through mobs of minions and henchmen, but who cares about peasants?) He never kills innocent victims, never accidentally kills the wrong person, and will let a mass-murderer escape to kill again rather than put women or children in the line of fire. In Bond's world there is no collateral damage.

Bond is a *gentleman*. He is a master of every form of hand-to-hand com-bat known to man, but his signature weapon (which has its own name, by the way) is a small-caliber pistol, or as Sir Alec Guinness might say, "A weapon with a more *civilized* edge." Bond always meets his adversaries face-to-face and challenges them to single combat; he never strikes first from hiding or without warning, and he would never call in an airstrike to level a crowded restaurant just to get the one evil man hiding in the basement. Bond's adventures frequently end with götterdämmerung final battles, true, but it's always left to a Felix Leiter or a Tiger Tanaka to do the scut-work of marshalling the faceless but loyal peasant infantry; Bond himself answers to a higher calling. In Bond's world there are no drunken and unreliable CIA mercenaries.

Finally, Bond is a *romantic*. As he travels on his journey, beautiful women are constantly throwing themselves at his feet, and while he may have dalliances—in some stories, *lots* of dalliances—there is always one true love waiting for him at the end of the tale. Admittedly the earlier stories of his adventures were often quite bawdy, but that was more a reflection of then-current social mores and the bawdiness has been toned down considerably in recent years. In Bond's world there are no sexually transmitted diseases or pregnant ex-girlfriends.

With all the evidence that has been presented, then, the answer finally begins to become clear. Who is James Bond? He's no *noir* anti-hero, no undercover operative, and no brilliant intelligence analyst. He's no government assassin, no cold-blooded killer, and certainly no spy.

What he is, in truth, is a *paladin*. He's a modern knight-errant who roams the world, righting wrongs, fighting evil, and protecting the weak. He's a *fantasy hero*, and the place he truly belongs is in the Land of Make-Believe and Should Have Been, standing shoulder to shoulder with Aragorn, Luke Skywalker, Sir Lancelot, Wilfred of Ivanhoe, and Roland and all his cavaliers, defending the borders of the peaceable kingdom from the never-resting forces of darkness that roam out there in the wild lands.

(P.S. And those of you who are still bothered by Bond's bawdiness should go back and read some of the early *chansons de geste*, *Orlando Furioso* or, for that matter, an unexpurgated version of *Canterbury Tales*. The early *aubades* and *tagelieder* in particular are just full of tales of heroic and noble knights who nonetheless are a rather randy lot and never pass up the chance for a good roll in the hay with an unhappily married noblewoman. The idea that medieval heroes were somehow pure and chaste is mostly the work of eighteenth-century bluenose Thomas Bowdler and his imitators, not an accurate reflection of the actual songs and tales of the Middle Ages.)

Does Bond Have a Place in the Modern World?

Finally, we come back to the question we began with: does Commander James Bond, C.M.G., R.N.V.R., have a useful place in the twenty-first century? The answer is yes, but for not the most comforting of reasons.

The truth of the matter is that *real* deep-cover human intelligence work is a very disturbing, unpleasant, and ugly business. The truth is that in the world of espionage, "truth" itself is a very rare commodity, constantly attended by a bodyguard of lies and veiled by a smokescreen of ambiguities. The truth is that assassinations and executions—those intelligence operations which are euphemistically termed "wet work" in the trade—are utterly stomach-turning in their hideousness and frequently result in much blood, screaming, and injury to innocent bystanders.

The irony—some might say the hypocrisy—of western civilization is that we *need* those modern paladins who walk the wild forests at the edge of the known world, slaying dragons and goblins so that the petit bourgeoisie might sleep soundly in their beds. But the truth of the matter is that a clear look at the *actions* of those same paladins will give most people the screaming heebie-jeebies.

And so we need Commander James Bond, Companion of the Order of St. Michael and St. George, Royal Navy Volunteer Reserve.

Or put it this way: If you want a sickeningly realistic and unblinking look at the world of real wet work, go watch actor Daniel Craig portray Mossad assassin "Alan" in the movie *Munich* (2005). But if you want a comforting heroic fantasy, go watch actor Daniel Craig portray James Bond in the movie *Casino Royale*.

Personally, I know which one *I* would rather go to sleep thinking about.

BRUCE BETHKE works, writes, and when time permits, lives in beautiful, mosquito-infested Minnesota. In some circles, he is best known for his 1980 short story "Cyberpunk." In others, he is better known for his Philip K. Dick Award–winning novel *Headcrash*. What very few people in either circle have known until recently is that he actually works for America's leading maker of supercomputers, and all his *best* science fiction gets repackaged as "futurism studies" and sold at stunningly inflated prices to various government agencies, where it is promptly stamped SECRET and filed away, never to be seen again.

Bethke can be contacted via his Web site at www.brucebethke.com.

Acknowledgments

Our grateful appreciation goes to Ajay Chowdhury, editor of *Kiss Kiss Bang Bang* magazine (www.007.info), and Matthew Newton of the Bond Film Informant (www.mjnewton.demon.co.uk/bond/), for their assistance with this manuscript.